KU-187-815

WITHDRAWN FROM STOCK

A Teacher's Guide

The Schools Council Environmental Studies Project
team have prepared four books to illustrate
their approach with children of the 5 to 13 age range:

A Teacher's Guide
Case Studies
Starting from Maps
Starting from Rocks

The members of the Project:
Melville Harris, director
Meurig Evans, deputy director
Gwenallt Rees
Douglas Myers
Stephen Moore, evaluator

This book was written by Melville Harris, Meurig Evans
and Gwenallt Rees

A Teacher's Guide

Schools Council Environmental Studies Project

Rupert Hart-Davis Educational Publications   London

23936

Granada Publishing Limited
First published in Great Britain 1972
by Rupert Hart-Davis Educational Publications Ltd
3 Upper James Street London W1R 4BP

Copyright © Schools Council Publications 1972

All rights reserved. No part of this publication
may be reproduced, stored in a retrieval system,
or transmitted, in any form or by any means,
electronic, mechanical, photocopying, recording
or otherwise, without the prior permission of
the publishers.

ISBN 0 247 54441 8

Filmset by Keyspools Ltd, Golborne, Lancs.
Printed and bound by C. Tinling & Co. Ltd, London and Prescot

Coláiste
Mhuire Gan Smál
Luimneach
Class No. 372·83
Acc. No. 38,644

Contents

1 The Nature of Environmental Studies

'Our Stone Circle'

My infant/junior school is situated in a typical built-up industrial valley in South Wales. Around it are all the features of a town that has developed through the exploitation of coal over the last 100 years — the houses, chapels, church, shops, library, mines and factories, the roads, canals and railways and the close, though mixed, community of people whose ancestors came from many parts of Britain.

The school, built in 1907 and containing box-like classrooms around a central hall, set in a concrete playground, caters for children in the four to eleven age range. It is reasonably well supplied with reference books and also boasts T.V., radio, a duplicator, tape recorders, a slide projector, a supply of O.S. maps, old photographs of the area and small scientific equipment.

In this setting, with a class of 31 children of mixed ability and aged nine to eleven years, we recently developed a study based upon an open park area within 300 metres of the school. This park was some time ago the site for the National Eisteddfod of Wales, an annual festival of music and literature. Wherever this festival is held a ring of stones called a Gorsedd Circle is left as a sign, and it was this circle that first started the interest of the class. The Gorsedd Park, a well-known feature of the town, was close to the school, was a safe place for the children to work in, and had a great variety of things in it that were likely to provide interests for the children who, the previous year, had studied the local canals, roads, the colliery and other local industries. We started off with a chat in the classroom about the park, part of which we could see from the school. We looked at our local 6 in. and 25 in. O.S. maps checking, from past experience, the distance of the park from the school, our homes, and other local points and also discussed why we were going and what we would need to take with us. Then with some clear orders on conduct, we set off carrying O.S. maps, compasses, tapes, clip boards, paper, pencils and a few empty biscuit tins.

At the park, as is usually the case, some children quickly noted things they would wish to study, or questions they would like to try to answer:

'Why should a circle of stones represent the Eisteddfod?'
'Who put them there?'

'How did they put them there?'
'Can we make a map of the park?'
'Can we find out about the trees?'

Other children, however, expressed little interest in anything that lay around them. To some of them it was a well-kept area to pass through on their way home, or a place for old people to sit in. With these children I had to take a more positive role suggesting, and in some cases giving, activities rather than topics. With the local O.S. map I did some orientation exercises relating the park to features including roads and the traffic moving alongside the park, and I posed some mathematical problems on the circumference and radius of the stone circle.

This short exploratory visit was useful and good fun, though perhaps the highlight for some children was when they gathered in the circle and made a mock sacrifice of one girl on the flat central stone! One girl thought this enormous stone 'a cold bed for a giant'!

Back in the classroom the possibilities were further discussed and, as a result of the children's suggestions and my purpose in using this approach, I prepared a small set of suggestion cards for the mixed ability and interest groups that were formed. These cards gave some specific instructions to the children so as to initiate work but also tried to provide for the children's natural interests. For example, the card for the plants group included:

1 Use the quadrat frame to discover how many different kinds of plants grow within 1 sq. metre inside the stone circle. Mark their positions on your squared paper.
2 Collect one specimen *only* of each plant.
3 How many plant types grow in 1 sq. metre underneath the branches of a large oak tree in the park?
4 Compare your results.
5 Make similar tests in other places of your own choice.

Similar cards were prepared for the groups studying roads, rocks, maps, and the village community.

On our next, more intensive, visit the whole class had some general activities to undertake, each group had more specialized activities, and opportunities were given and time allowed for individual interests to develop. Throughout the activities I tried to ensure closer observation and controlled collecting of what lay in the park and the recording of features in a variety of ways, including mapping by a group who prepared a simple transect, precise plan making through detailed measuring of the circle, tabular recording by the plant and traffic groups, and use of grid references and labelling by the soils group.

Through these activities the groups gathered enough data and material for classroom follow-up to continue. Much of this initial work was of a scientific nature. Soil samples from the park and the children's homes were tested, attempts were made to calculate the total weight of stones in the circle, traffic flow was represented graphically and the differences between flowering and non-flowering plants were studied. An un-expected but fruitful line of study arose when two boys in moving a litter bin uncovered a circle of yellow grass — an incident that started off tests on 'green in nature'. The children reported on their activities to the rest of the class — usually emphasizing their methods of working, the instruments they had used and the conclusions they had reached, rather than the information they had read about their topics.

Many of the children were unaware of the origins and nature of the festival represented by the stone circle. A local resident came and showed us a 16 mm colour film of some of the Eisteddfod ceremonies that had taken place in this stone circle in 1953. It was a source of wonder, and no small amusement, for many children to see their parents on film in a year long before they themselves were born. With the help of this film I outlined the growth of the festival and the significance of its ceremonies for the whole class. Further activities then developed — the children organised poetry and prose competitions which all could enter, biographical accounts of poets and musicians with local connections were produced and Morning Services based upon their lives and works were prepared. The ceremonies themselves were very attractive to the children so they rehearsed them before going to the park to perform the ceremonies and dance within the circle itself.

Thoughts of other places where similar circles have been set up led children to write to a school in a North Wales town where the Eisteddfod had recently been held and also to organizers of ceremonies in Ireland, Scotland, Cornwall and Brittany. The postman was soon greeted with particular attention as letters began to arrive from pen-pals, home and foreign newspapers, and interested people from other countries. Routes followed by letters were studied and outlines of the main road and rail networks of Britain produced.

Apart from the class and group activities, individual interests were aroused, the value of which I cannot estimate. I realize as a teacher that I can rarely expect to see the final results of this work. One boy appears to have developed a great, perhaps lasting, interest in foreign languages through the letters we received from Brittany, and another developed a rock collecting craze after a visit we made to the quarry that provided the stones for 'our circle'.

For me the study was a continuation of the means I use to give my children practice in observation of the physical world around them and an increasing awareness of the society in which they live. The way they worked, their interest as the study evolved and their pride when the tape and slide record of the work was shown to their parents, further convinces me that this was time well spent in an enjoyable and purposeful manner.

For many children throughout Britain activities similar to those described in this study are a formal part of school life at infant, junior, middle and lower secondary level. The precise purpose of the work varies with the age and ability of the children but at all stages from five to thirteen years the guiding principle is of an approach based upon direct observation of the environment of school and home.

This approach is called 'environmental studies' by an increasing number of teachers who recognize its value as part of the total curriculum of their schools. The principle is not new in education, though its implementation has new elements that make the approach particularly important at the present time. This book sets out one approach based on detailed work with teachers in 230 schools throughout England and Wales. Other methods of using environmental studies may be preferred by individual teachers or schools.

A Subject View

Environmental Studies is here regarded as an approach to a curriculum field rather than a subject to be taught to children of primary and middle school age. The relevance of environmental studies as a 'subject' for five to thirteen-year-olds is difficult to maintain. Any academic subject has at least two main character-istics — a body of knowledge and a particular method of enquiry. The fields of information into which environmental studies can take children are so extensive that the information content cannot be defined. And on practical grounds the potential information material is so extensive that it is beyond one person's comprehension.

The range of concepts related to environmental studies also raises problems of definition. The concept of total environment is difficult to define; 'ecology' embraces so much, and straddles so many disciplines. However, key features such as those of structure, change and location can be specified.

The definition of the method of enquiry is a less difficult undertaking though this too has its problems. The development of precise methods of making direct observations and recordings of physical and social phenomena, the conduct of physical and social experiments, and the communication of the results are characteristics of the method employed. Workers in many different subjects use this enquiry-based method in their studies. The difficulties of finding a unique definition of environ-mental studies shows how awkward a field of study it is for young children. The approach to the curriculum on a subject basis is itself open to question. Young children used to the environment as an integrated whole will not have developed the concept of subject divisions. Activities gradually lead to a growing awareness of the conventional divisions that can be given to knowledge, thus leading to more complex specializations.

An environmental studies field sharply divided into subjects would pay little attention to the way in which children view their world. What is needed is an approach which helps them to see more clearly what lies around them and introduces a variety of methods of studying and communicating their obser-vations. As such, environmental studies can make a significant contribution within the total curriculum of young children, without making irrelevant claims to subject status at this stage.

The Curriculum

The curriculum in most primary schools is organized to include a number of clearly defined though overlapping fields of study. Some middle schools and the lower end of many secondary schools continue this general principle though examples of finely-divided curricula also exist. Where subject-divided curricula are devised for children from the age of eleven, or from nine as in some middle schools, a valid environmental studies approach cannot be implemented. Thus it is the curriculum built around a number of broad fields of study which is here considered relevant.

The main concerns of the curriculum are language, mathematics, the creative arts and religious and physical education. Alongside these has existed a less well-defined field expressed by a wide variety of names including 'topics', 'projects', 'centres of interest', 'social studies', 'geography — history — science' and, increasingly 'environmental studies'. These terms do not refer to studies whose boundaries exactly correspond but they generally represent 'people, places and things'. In order of priority within the curriculum these studies lie below the basic functions of literacy and numeracy and have consequently generally been stunted and imprecise.

The over-riding importance of language and mathematical skills as the bases of selection for secondary education have frequently led to a didactic teaching method aimed at producing formal competence. The teaching methods used for the 'basics' have usually been applied to other studies as well, with the result that these have been concerned with giving or collecting of information on a variety of topics and recording it in a written or oral form. Because of this concentration on a limited range of methods many topics and projects have ended as factual written accounts illustrated by drawings or cut-outs from magazines.

Fortunately, this is not universal. Individual teachers have for decades developed in their children scientific and artistic skills in addition to the basic ones of language and mathematics. Notable examples exist of local studies undertaken by children under the guidance of gifted teachers, but these are exceptions.

In the last decades, however, the general picture has altered due to changes in British education and the growth of the mass-media. As the controlling influence of the selection examinations at 11+ have weakened, many teachers have tried to extend the range of their curricula, sometimes of their own volition, but often encouraged by local advisory staffs and members of Her Majesty's Inspectorate of Schools. Though the development of language skills has been kept as the main requirement many attempts have been made to broaden the scope of primary school activities.

These changes have taken place because of the wide variety of information, expressed in many forms, that has become available to children in modern society. Before the development of the mass-media, especially television, communication for the majority of people was largely through written, or spoken, language. Therefore the ability to read and write were especially emphasized in school. Today however, children of all ages are presented with information in a variety of pictorial, diagrammatic and cartographical forms. It has thus become essential for schools to provide curricula which can develop the ability to use and interpret these forms of communication. This can be achieved by an environmental studies approach.

The Field of Environmental Studies
If, in the study of the Stone Circle, the investigations and results had been communicated only through traditional basic skills, the children's different activities would have provided good exercises in language and art. However, the account shows that the approach used required a more extensive range of skills.

These skills involve collecting and classifying all types of physical and social data; formulating and conducting tests and experiments; mapping; interpreting photographs and sketches; and the preparation and presentation of interviews and question-naires. These 'study skills' have traditionally been given only limited attention with children below thirteen years of age, but need to play an increasingly significant role in schools.

The attention given to these skills has been limited for several reasons. For example, they have not been featured in selection examinations for secondary education. There are also indications that some teachers have wrongly assumed that children have an intuitive understanding of photographs, maps, sketches and diagrams. It has been thought that these activities were suitable only for children at secondary school. Greater knowledge of the development of logical thinking in children gained from research, such as the Nuffield Junior Science Project, has shown this view to be unjustified for most children. Often teachers at primary schools have felt that their training has not equipped them to cope with this field of the curriculum. The development in Colleges of Education courses, and the expansion of in-service provisions are helping to overcome this problem.

Although these study skills are the core of an environmental studies approach, they cannot develop in isolation. Written and spoken language permeate the environmental studies field. Until children have developed reading and writing to the level where they can be used for pleasure and understanding, the growth of study skills will be very limited. Environmental studies should in no way reduce language standards of children. On the contrary they should make precision of language an even greater need, and direct contact with the environment should provide stimulation for creative expression. Likewise, many opportunities for mathematical activities should arise.

This curriculum field should also help the growth of social skills. The growth of responsibility and initiative, the ability to fit in with a group, the giving and accepting of criticism, and respect for people and the physical environment can all be helped by the activities in this approach.

The Study Skills
Though the development of the study skills is the main objective of environmental studies, there are other objectives as well. But the skills that are peculiar to this approach are identified first.

Mapping   The skills involved in making, reading and inter-preting maps and plans form one group. They are of particular value to children as they provide a special medium for study and expression of the world around them. In making use of maps a child must develop the ability to draw accurate outlines of features, to take linear and angular measurements and to use analytical techniques which involve co-ordinates and other methods of location (fig. 11). These practical activities can provide the concepts of scale, direction, and co-ordinates as well as the more general concept of location itself. Through a variety of studies over a period of time, a child can develop a more precise understanding of his location with reference to his local and wider environments, and also have at his disposal a tool for studying the inter-relationships within the environment.

Classifying   Another group of skills are those associated with collecting, classifying and identifying material and data. Different types of physical material and abstract data require different collecting processes. Specialized equipment, though often of a simple nature, may be required to gather insects and trap small creatures. Questionnaires, tables and maps are necessary for the accumulation of social statistics; outline sketches may be needed for recording architectural or historical remains; and bags and other containers will be necessary for collecting flowers and stones. The construction and use of this equipment, simple and complex, covers a wide field. Random collections of leaf specimens will precede quadrat counts (fig. 12); simple lists of survey questions will come before sampling methods of collecting social data; and large scale plans and models of small areas will anticipate small scale transects of large areas. All of these activities are geared to careful observation, collecting and recording of the raw material upon which children can practise classification and identification.

The processes of grouping the material are many and varied, and must be related to the ability of the children. Simple activities using apparatus such as hoops to separate the physical specimens may be followed by the drawing of venn-diagrams using descriptive criteria. More difficult groupings based on multiple criteria requiring a list of specified tests and examinations on the material can follow later. The building of simple keys and the later use of more advanced identification tables are important to these activities, though the need to name specimens should not be over-emphasized.

Experimenting   Associated with the classificatory skills are the skills required for experiments. The formulation, conduct and interpretation of simple and complex experiments are desirable, though difficult, activities for young children. The posing of questions requiring tests in order to provide answers is frequently encountered in work of this type, though the questions often arise as a result of leading by the teacher.

Children need to have repeated opportunities for practising these procedures before the answers satisfy them. Few variables can be involved in tests though the number will increase as the children's experience develops. Through practical involvement in experiments children begin to develop control, the powers of criticism, the need for measurement and the suspension of judgement.

'In one of the folk songs it was said that water used to wash a horse's hooves would wash clothes cleaner than ordinary water. Some of the girls tried to find out if this was true. One of the fathers, who owned a garage, made a small, hand-operated washing machine and the girls brought a large white sheet to school. The sheet was put in a bucket full of tea and a mixture of red clay and water, after which it was dried and then cut into thirty-two equal parts. One piece was washed for three minutes in one pint of clean, boiling water. Another piece was washed under the same conditions except that the water used had been brought along by one of the children and had been previously used to wash the hooves of his horse. It was discovered that the folk song was correct for the second piece was much cleaner than the first. The girls then went on to compare all the washing powders they could find making certain that the conditions remained the same for each sample. They recorded their results and used them as a list of the "best buys" for their parents.'

In this example the idea of control was well developed. For the children it appeared that the pieces of cloth were equal in size, quality and dirtiness. Apart from the nature of the water, they were subjected to identical washing conditions. Thus, logically they could claim that it was washing the horse's hooves in the water that gave the difference in cleanliness to the cloth.

Adults can recognize the complications of providing absolute controls in this example. Was the sheet of uniform quality? Was it equally dirty all over? Was the water always at the same temperature? Was it something else in the water that provided the result? All these more sophisticated queries did not arise at the children's level — and if they had, the problems thus posed might have been beyond the capabilities of the children to solve.

As it was, at their level, these children had an opportunity to develop their understanding of experimental conditions. It was the activity rather than the result that was significant; and with greater experience more refined experimental conditions could be developed by the children.

Questionnaires   Methods of conducting interviews and making surveys through questionnaires are of growing importance in modern society where planning requires statistical information. The skills involved in these activities have not yet been introduced in any marked degree to young children in British schools. Any environmental study of an area must concern itself with the people as well as the place. The development of the tools for gathering information about the social environment becomes one of the objects. It is not to be expected that young children of less than thirteen years of age can conduct interviews with the expertise of a trained adult interviewer. To turn children loose to question the local populace is to invite problems. A series of graded steps where children interview their friends, their teachers, the caretaker and so on can help to develop the confidence, adaptability and accuracy that interviews demand.

Along with the development of interviewing skills, children can learn the principles involved in constructing questionnaires. The type of information needed should be considered when making a list of questions for interviewing a classmate. At a later stage, attention must be given to the ethical problems of asking people for personal information, as well as sampling and interpreting statistical data. Ill-organized questions to the public by children having no experience usually lead to time-wasting.

Photographs and Sketches   Yet another form of particular skill is the use of sketches and photographs. Annotating sketches to isolate significant features of landscapes, buildings, styles of dress or biological specimens is an essential skill especially when used in conjunction with photographs. The great increase of information in pictorial form in modern society makes it essential that children be given opportunities to examine photographs as sources of information and evidence as well as illustrations of verbal statements. Of particular value are activities requiring comparison of illustrations of one area at different stages in time.

Basic Skills

None of the study skills that have been outlined exists in isolation. The results of studying an area through maps are generally expressed in spoken or written language. Experiments and social surveys are ultimately expressed in words or figures. Studies of the changes of an area usually require writing and illustrations for the children to represent their final descriptions or conclusions. Thus, the study skills generally require that children possess facility in language and mathematics, basic skills which are themselves enhanced by use in these activities. Accurate and concise reporting of factual information is an essential element in environmental studies. The increasing ability of children to use language for describing the processes involved in their studies is one of the significant outcomes of the work.

'Yesterday at half past one, our class went to Valley Pool. We got there in about a quarter of an hour and when I was about two hundred yards from the pool I stopped to sketch it. It was quite cold down there so we were glad we had taken our coats. Simon and his group were finding the width of the pool by reflection, but we were using quadrats to see if there was any difference between the plant types at the edge of the pool and those further away. . . .'

In such direct reporting, the importance of accuracy in spelling, punctuation and general grammar should be emphasized and all mistakes corrected.

This does not mean that the first-hand experiences should not be taken as opportunities for children to express themselves more personally.

The City from Dundry

The vast and hazy city
A Giant's favourite toy
Tiny houses like matchboxes
Stand neatly in their rows
Like thousands of ants,
Their roof tops gleaming
Red and brown
And windows flash and wink
Reflecting silvery light.

Flats, small to me, tower
Above the houses;
Miniature tall buildings
Ruling the land.
Cars like Corgi toys
Skim the grey roads
Vast patches of darkness
Slide across the sky at high speed.

They float across the city
Like pieces of cotton wool
On a shiny surface of blue
A few pigeons fly over the houses
Like stray clouds
A shadow covers the heart of the City.

From far up on the hill,
It's quiet and still
An expanse of brickwork
Pushes through the countryside
With thousands of Churches!

Prose, poetry, drama and painting may be used to express the impressions and aesthetic appreciation arising out of excursions into city, town and country. Perceptive teachers make use of such opportunities without necessarily involving themselves in the wider range of environmental studies.

Social Skills

Inside and outside of school, children are involved in situations where social attitudes are learnt and maturing takes place. An environmental studies approach bridging the boundaries between schools and a wider environment has a particular contribution to make in this sphere.

Within the class, discussion and the organization of children into groups requires the development of individual and group behaviour. Unless discussions are orderly, their value is limited. Children must accept that it is necessary to take one's turn in discussion as in many other activities. One of the objectives of an approach of this type is to develop children's ability to fit in with groups of their peers, to give and accept comments and criticisms and to conduct themselves in an acceptable manner. These social skills take on an added significance when children undertake studies outside the school estate. On excursions, respect for the welfare and safety of the public must be insisted on by teachers. For example, the children should leave space for other pedestrians on pavements and approach people courteously when asking for information. The physical environment in town and country should be respected by following the Countryside Code and avoiding dropping litter.

Such instructions have a restrictive element in them, but they are important in an educational approach aimed at developing awareness and appreciation of the physical and social environments. The quality of our future environment will depend upon attitudes of concern and respect — attitudes that an environmental studies approach can help to mould.

The Progression of Skills
It is generally accepted that most children, with practice and increasing maturity, progressively improve their language and mathematical skills. Standardized tests in these skills have long been in existence, specifying the age norms of performance for children.

Study skills also show this feature of progression, though information on age norms is more limited than in the language and mathematics field. These skills are being subjected to increasingly detailed examination, as in the Bristol Achievement Tests produced by A. Brimer and published by Thomas Nelson & Sons Ltd.

The different skills involved can be shown to exist at simple and advanced levels, though stages in the progression are often difficult to specify. The specification of the possible grades of attainment in certain skills is one of the aims of the Schools Council Environmental Studies Project. Through the identification of the significant skills and their development a feasible framework for study of the environment can be established.

The skills of map production and reading depend upon many factors including a child's physical ability to handle paper, pencil and other more sophisticated tools. His previous experience of mapping and his grasp of the concepts of a map, direction, scale, angular measurement and co-ordinates have also to be considered.

At the ability level of the child the resultant map may be a freehand sketch where map and picture intermingle with no consistent relationship to scale, direction or distribution. On the other hand it may be an accurately drawn, scale-contoured map of an extensive area with conventional symbols and key, grid and title to allow interpretations to be made. Between these levels, with children of the five to thirteen age range, several stages can exist, as illustrated in *Starting from Maps*.

Progression of another order is to be found in the development of classificatory systems by children. A variety of methods whereby materials can be ordered at simple and complex levels must be made available to the child. The example outlined in *Starting from Rocks* illustrates that the first groupings by children are often on the basis of one criterion such as colour. Specimens are sorted physically or by a variety of representations in graphs, numbers and diagrams. Further examinations, with increasing maturity, show this simple division to be unsatisfactory so activities involving the construction of Venn diagrams, for hardness and lime content, the introduction of sampling techniques, and the use of more complex diagrammatic forms become necessary.

The ability to classify materials can be improved if children have frequent opportunities to organize collections of many kinds of physical material and abstract data according to self-derived and conventional criteria. It is doubtful if all children improve their skills of classification in the same sequential pattern, just as it is also doubtful if all children can attain the higher levels of complex classification.

Devising experiments to answer particular problems or questions is a frequent requirement in environmental studies. Often, when attempting to classify objects, simple tests become necessary to compare one property of the materials studied. As activities continue, the problems of dealing with further variables arise and ways of control are sought, as in the example of the horse's hooves. Much more research is necessary to clarify the stages whereby children may progress to the level of constructing control experiments to test hypotheses they have suggested.

As indicated earlier, there is also an increasing complexity in the ways of producing and examining sketches, photographs and questionnaires. The scale of skills ranges from the simple annotation of sketches and photographs representing single items to the detailed analysis of landscape sketches or aerial photographs covering wide areas. On the basis of the study skills specified and the approximate lines of their progression, schools can provide practical situations for children to interpret the world around them.

Concepts in Environmental Studies

In emphasizing the study skills there is no suggestion that their development by children is the end purpose of environmental studies. Skills can be little more than manipulative exercises unless they lead to an understanding of the principles underlying the actions. The study skills are regarded as the practical activities which enable children to produce situations and instruments for the collecting, organization and examination of data, and its final interpretation and representation. Through such activities, applied in a variety of situations over a long period of time, children can develop the general concepts which bring greater order to their personal views of their environments.

The range of concepts involved in environmental studies is very great and few children are likely to develop the full spectrum. However, certain key concepts, such as those of location, class and change in the environment should be developed within the limits of the capability of a child.

Activities based on the general concept of inclusion or class formation can lead to an understanding of class. This understanding may range from the simplest level of resemblance when a child groups two objects that are alike in some way, through the level of multiple class membership when it is clear that objects can be classed in different categories, to the higher levels when classes can be recognized in a hierarchical pattern. A child can reach his appropriate stage in this conceptual framework through the development and use of study skills.

Another logical structure that a child can be helped to develop is that concerned with his location in the physical world. Through activities involving maps, plans, profiles and photographs a child becomes increasingly aware of spatial distributions. The growth of an understanding of time and chronology, and change leading to growth and decay, should also form a part of an environmental studies approach.

The Role of the Environment

One of the main objectives of this approach is the development of ways of studying and understanding, and the environment should be seen as a vehicle helping to achieve this.

Study skills have traditionally been developed, usually within specialist subjects, at secondary level inside the classroom. This has often been in a formal teaching situation with little opportunity for first hand investigation. A similar approach might be considered for younger children where physical materials could be brought into the classroom, together with work books and programmed texts of various forms. Information about the immediate and more distant localities and times could be provided at second-hand and strategies for the development of study skills devised.

Such an approach may have its attractions but children learn most effectively by personal experience; therefore an approach based on direct investigation of the immediate locality of the school is of greater value, though second-hand material can be used at later stages.

At infant school the environment within the school estate should be structured to provide as wide a range of experiences as possible. Variations of colour, texture, form and sound, the presence of living plants and animals and the availability of a wide range of materials are normal features of good infant schools. Often children are taken outside the school to provide them with a wider range of experiences and in some cases large-scale models of the locality are constructed by pupils and teachers, often helped by parents.

The varied, interesting environment is provided as a stimulus for the development of the basic skills of language and number and the expression of creativity in many forms. Many of the stimuli can be encountered only outside the school, for it is only in their natural situations that many of the objects can be perceived in the correct context of place, shape, sound and other characteristics.

'We walked along the tow path until we came to an old empty building. Then it began to rain so, having first made sure it was safe, I decided we should take shelter there. It was cold and dark and the building smelt musty. Everywhere was draped with cobwebs and was very dirty. What a stimulus for the adventure stories the children wrote later.'

Such incidents as this one, taken from an account of a study of a short length of canal, cannot be reproduced in the classroom. The children involved were given an experience which they later tried to communicate through language and the other tools they had available. The environment should be regarded at this stage as a reservoir of varied experiences. Many of the incidents will arise fortuitously, but visits to a varied range of sites can provide an awareness of people, places and things, and the beauty and squalor that exist in everyone's environment.

Later, in primary school, when a firm base of language ability has been established, the environment can be regarded as a vehicle for a range of study skills.

Children need to be placed in situations where they meet the realities of the environment and where they can see for themselves buildings of different types, various plants and animals, the volume of motor and pedestrian traffic, the length of a hundred metres of road, and the colours, designs and textures that exist all around them. By expressing these perceptions in words, sketches, maps, graphs and diagrams they can develop an understanding of the features and the forms in which they have been represented. Then they are able to make full use of the material they find. Studies based on direct investigation of the environment provide concrete operations through which the transition to more abstract levels of thinking can be made.

The most significant aspect of this approach is that it is both purposeful and enjoyable. The existence of this work within the general curriculum adds variety to the overall pattern of school work. Children enjoy themselves when they are interested and involved rather than when they have little to do. It is a mistaken idea that all children are immediately interested in a study of their environment — many often show very little interest in the initial stages of studies, and the teacher often has to be the motivating force. In most cases, however, when investigating the total environment with its colours, sound and movements, and when attempting to answer specific questions, children's involvement is marked, their enthusiasms grow and their interest remains.

For children in the upper range of the five to thirteen age group, the use of the environment takes on a somewhat different role. After earlier experience of environmental studies they will have developed some competence. Subject specializations exist for many children especially from the age of thirteen, and elements of these specializations may begin to assume greater significance within the environmental studies framework. The methods, tools used and attitudes developed in an environmental studies approach are those which are particularly relevant to historians, geographers, scientists and sociologists. As children's ability for abstract reasoning increases, and as the skills they use become more complex, the growth of specialization can be an acceptable progression. It may, however, be seen as a disintegration of the environmental studies approach into separate subjects within which particular skills and knowledge are significant.

In preparation for such divisions, a greater emphasis on the subject elements in terms of information and concepts can be introduced to the studies. A local historical site may intentionally be used as a starting-point to study a 'patch' of history; contrasting plant growth in a lane may lead to generalizations on aspect and other ecological features; and contrasting land use in a valley transect may serve to illustrate regional contrasts within a world framework.

There may well be other alternatives to subject specializations for pupils over the age of thirteen years. The continuation of inter-related studies of an environmental studies type into secondary school may be advantageous for some pupils. It is not our purpose here to elaborate on the nature of such courses, though teachers concerned for children undertaking environmental studies in the eleven to thirteen age group need to consider the alternative possibilities of single subjects or integrated courses.

Thus, the role of the environment as a resource for learning is seen to vary with the age and ability of the children involved. In the early school years it is used as a stimulus for the basic skills; later it provides the practical situation through which study skills can be developed and finally it provides local examples for specialist or integrated subjects.

Social Awareness
A further aim of an environmental studies approach is the development by children of an awareness and appreciation of the society within which they live. Modern society, especially with the growth of the mass-media, tends to emphasize the exotic rather than the local, and the general rather than the

particular, in such a way that the significance of the place and society within which the child lives may be diminished in his eyes. Yet it is within the local context that he exists, and it is surrounded by familiar places and people that he grows. A clearer view of this social environment is essential for a child who can only grow to his full stature to the extent that he is introduced to the culture of the community in which he lives, to the extent that he is allowed and enabled to experience it as something dynamic which has to be preserved, enriched and transmitted to those who come after'.

Much of our cultural heritage is preserved in oral and written accounts which can bring some awareness of his roots to a child, but greater vividness and reality can be brought to it by his seeing evidence of changes that have occurred.

A girl aged eleven, having visited an old cottage which had been closely associated with the Chartists movement, wrote:

'This is the Cottage which was once a woollen mill. We have written a great deal about the history of this house in our notes. We spoke to Mrs. —— who now lives there, who told us the looms were originally on the top floor of the house . . . the colourful waistcoats worn by the Chartists in the 19th Century were made at the cottage. We have written about these Chartists and made a list of the six points they wanted in their charter. Because of their efforts we all now have a greater say in the government of our town and country. When we hear how these Chartists suffered to enable more people to get a vote it is strange to think that so many people never bother to use their vote at election times today.'

The environment of a school is much more than a collection of features that can be subjected to various processes of study. For many children it is the area which is the centre of existence for them and their families. To subject that area to study, to assess the physical and cultural quality of the place where they live, to consider changes that may be advisable and to relate the area to the wider environments of the world are activities that should be an element in all curricula.

There will inevitably be considerable contrasts in opportunities for such involvement because of accidents of location. Schools in the middle of large housing estates will not generally have many remnants of social history to hand, whereas schools in some ancient towns may be surrounded by physical evidence of change and continuity. The task of the teachers, as suggested later, is more difficult in some environments than in others, but within the limits of the school and its surroundings such studies should be undertaken.

The general concern for the quality of environments is likely to give opportunities to appreciate the beauty and squalor to be seen in many places. Whether the aesthetic impressions are expressed in drawing, painting, collage, modelling or language, the opportunities for heightened perception through direct contact with the world need to be taken.

Information

Experience has shown that many teachers, though accepting the value of an environmental studies approach, are concerned over the question of information that can be imparted through such studies. One teacher expressed this graphically by saying 'There are some six-inch nails of Welsh History that I believe it my duty to impart to the children in my school.'

It is clear that no environmental study can proceed without facts being gathered by children in a variety of ways. Information is gained in the field by observation or questioning and in the classroom there is constant use of references of all types. Great quantities of information are thus gathered and organized as part of the general conduct of environmental studies. Information is the raw material of the studies.

What cannot be specified is the particular information that will be found interesting or relevant to the investigations undertaken. Children may be fully involved in purposeful studies without concerning themselves with any 'six-inch nails' of specific information thought to be of particular significance and importance by the teacher. It is highly unlikely that over a period of years children studying different aspects of their environment will not become involved in many items related to incidents, personalities or features that are significant to them. However, no guarantee can, or should, be given that this situation will be reached.

The information field open to children engaged in enquiring is unlimited, and specifying the information considered by the teacher to be relevant turns enquiry into a farce. An active enquiry-based approach is not consistent with the children's gaining a specified body of information.

At the same time it needs to be recognized that the approach is not exclusive. It does not set out to claim that the whole curriculum should be covered in this way, but that it forms an important approach to a curriculum field.

If, within the curriculum field, a teacher is satisfied that there is certain essential information that children must obtain, then he will ensure that they gain it by some approach other than that of environmental studies. Where the amount of essential information is limited, the space it will take in the overall time available may allow an environmental studies approach to be introduced, but if the body of fact is very extensive it is unlikely that this will occur.

2 The Potential of School Environments

The first chapter dealt with the value of an environmental studies approach for children aged five to thirteen years. This chapter outlines some of the preliminary steps to be undertaken by the headteacher and staff when developing the approach in a school. The advice is based on the experiences of the Schools Council Curriculum Development team, with the co-operation of 230 schools in England and Wales. No single model applicable to all schools is suggested, but some general lines of organization adaptable for most school situations are described in detail.

What is a School Environment?
For any school, the environment available for direct investigation poses a number of practical difficulties. The age and mobility of the children, the location of the school and transport facilities have to be considered before any organized use of the environment can be undertaken. The problems of fatigue, maintaining interest and the ever-present toilet requirements of young children must be considered. Long walks to chosen locations often result in children arriving tired and confused, and neither the work on site nor the classroom follow-up is satisfactory. Experience suggests that trips should usually be confined to a fifteen-minute walk. A good general guide is to limit excursions to one hour, so that immediate follow-up work in the classroom is possible.

Within the limits imposed by fifteen minutes' walking distance, there should be numerous environmental features to serve as starting-points. There will have to be some selection of usable material. Many factories and some docks will not accept visits from young children; some sites such as abattoirs may be avoided for reasons of sensitivity; certain roads or junctions may be too dangerous for studies; some types of work may be too complex for children to understand. Every school environment is unique and as a learning resource needs to be known in detail by the staff.

A much wider environment can be used for direct investigation if transport is available, particularly where areas lack variety in their surroundings. The transport may be used for short half-day or day excursions or for week-end or longer stays at field centres, or other schools. Short excursions could be treated as extensions of the normal school environment and longer visits should contrast with the home locality.

Though more children today have the opportunity of visiting places far from their homes, the majority spend most of their school life in their local school. Therefore, this home area must be the main place for environmental studies, with occasional visits to more distant areas.

It is not usually possible at this stage for children to study at first-hand the wider environment of the country and the world. But having studied the local environment they are better equipped to undertake such studies.

The Local Potential

Every school has its own environment no matter where it is located (figs. 1–5); and it is through this environment that children will develop the basic study and social skills. Before introducing environmental studies into the curriculum an analysis of the school area may be made by the staff. The 'School Environment Profile Schedule' might be of use in such an analysis.

School Environment Profile Schedule

Type of School Area

1 School near the centre of a town or city.
2 School on a large estate.
3 School in a residential area near a city edge.
4 School in a small, old town.
5 A village school.
6 A school serving a scattered rural area.

Possible Starting Points

For study within fifteen minutes' walk, or transport, from school.

1 *Features allowing for the development of locational skills*
  (a) A variety of buildings of different design, constructed of various materials and performing different functions, *e.g.* school, shops, houses, chapels, factories, etc.
  (b) A variety of road or street types where observations of traffic and pedestrians can be made in safety.
  (c) A variety of rural and urban land use features.
  (d) Level land, hill slopes.
  (e) Features which can lead to the examination of similar aspects, *e.g.* rivers, roads, airports, docks in an ever-widening environment.

2 *Features allowing for the development of experimental and classificatory skills*
   (a) A range of plants and trees for controlled collection from a park, field, hillside, lane, waterside, etc.
   (b) A variety of living creatures in either their natural, domesticated or captive state, *e.g.* wild birds, farm animals, school pets, insects, zoo animals, pond or river creatures.
   (c) A variety of land surfaces, *e.g.* quarries, mountain screes, beach, cliff giving examples of rocks and fossils.
   (d) A range of essential services such as gas, electricity and water permitting an examination of the product through its various stages.

3 *Features allowing for the development of the concept of change*
   (a) Buildings around which communities have developed, *e.g.* fort, castle, church, factory, mine, etc.
   (b) A range of man-made links of communication, *e.g.* Roman road, drovers road, canal, rail, road, airport, docks.
   (c) A supply of documents, including old maps and photographs of the locality.
   (d) The presence in the locality of a wide age range of buildings showing, for example, the development of windows, roofing materials, etc.
   (e) The availability in the area of a museum, library, or public records office.
   (f) Evidence of the presence of domestic crafts, or occupations, of the past, *e.g.* mills, old implements and tools, clothes, gravestones, etc.
   (g) Old inhabitants of the area whose accounts of the past can be tape-recorded.

This schedule sets out some of the useful features of an environment. The first group of features may involve children in plan and map work of different grades of complexity. Single buildings such as the school itself, a shop, a church or a factory provide for simple activities involving measuring and making large-scale plans and sketches. More complex maps are possible where a variety of buildings or rural features are close together. The recognition by the teacher of the variety of features that can be recorded in map form is essential. For older children the slopes and hills in the locality are useful aids for recording heights on maps. Finally, mapping river, road, rail and other systems links the locality with the wider environment.

When assessing the value of the environment the staff should consider all the possibilities it offers for active, interesting study. A row of almost identical houses is of limited interest, whereas an area including houses, gardens, a playground, some shops and a factory opens up possibilities. Every school environment has some locations with greater potential than others, and only an examination of the locality can make this apparent.

Some of the second group of features, serving as starting points for collecting, classifying, identifying and experimenting, will also exist in, or near many schools. Children may well find many interests in a city park, but the range of possible interests will be greater if the teacher chooses an area which he knows has a variety of features but which is not too complex. There is an element of selectivity by the teacher but this is inevitable since not all parts of the environment are equally productive. In addition to the examination of plant and animal life, it is desirable to make use of opportunities to study power sources and essential services.

The features in the final group are particularly useful with regard to the concept of social change. Features of historical change can be found in many school areas. In some cases the changes may be seen in architectural features and building materials, but often the evidence is only documentary and oral. A knowledge of such documents and of their availability is an important part of the preparation for environmental studies.

Every school can provide a profile which illustrates the potential of the area. Teachers who know their area well will be encouraged to look at it from a new point of view, and those who do not will be provided with guidelines that they can use, at least until they become familiar with the area within which their children live. In addition, the profile can give guidance to new teachers and thus help overcome the increasing problem of changing staffs.

Figure 1. An old primary school in an industrial village. A varied environment easily available

Figure 2. A rural environment. Small schools in beautiful country, but the town is far away

Figure 3. A small school serving a scattered habitat. Varied countryside but urban studies are limited by distance

Figure 4. The decaying environment of a city school. A dangerous, though interesting, environment helped by a nearby park

Figure 5. A large school in a municipal estate. An apparently monotonous environment which in fact has considerable potential for studies

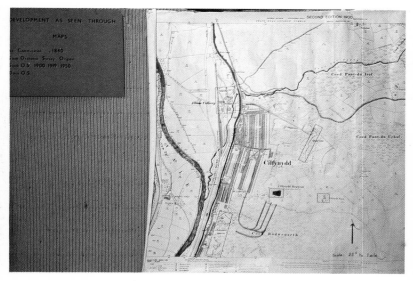

Figure 6. Potential study areas pin-pointed on a 25″ map of a school environment

7. En route, in safety, to the study
ear a town school
8. On location. Town children on a
s field course in North Wales

Figure 9. Where most environmental
studies work is done – in the classroom
Figure 10. A variety of skills being used by
groups developing a study. The teacher is
always near at hand

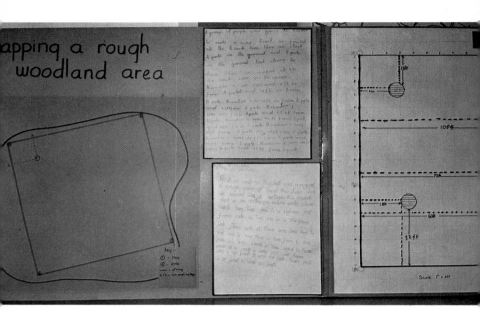

Figure 11. Information recorded by maps and plans as part of the growth of locational skills

Figure 12. Sampling and identification activities to aid the development of skills of classification

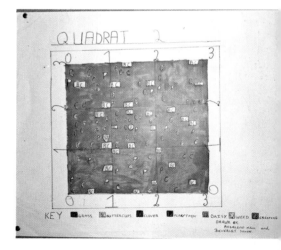

Figure 13. Crafts of the past represented
by large scale illustrations as an aid to the
growing awareness of change
Figure 14. Children involved in
constructive changes in the environment.
Planning and building a pool and a rockery
in a primary school

Figure 15. The finished pool and
surrounds. Safety is always a problem
Figure 16. An elaborate rose garden and
rockery made by pupils in a large secondary
comprehensive school

School Environment Profiles

The profiles produced by school staffs will reflect marked differences in environments. However, examination of a large number of school situations does suggest that certain environment types can be specified. Examples of these types are:

Urban Environments

1 A school in or near the centre of a large city. Problems of safety and lack of environmental variety are considerable and many social difficulties arise with pupils.

2 A school in a rapidly built residential estate catering for the post war population boom and slum clearance. There is generally a lack of variety in these environments and only limited social and open space areas for study.

3 A school in a well established residential area in city and town suburbs with fairly easy contact with rural areas or parks.

4 A school in a long-established small town with a wide range of social and physical starting points for study.

Rural Environments

5 A school serving a well-established closely-knit village community.

6 A school serving a scattered rural community.

The first four are the types of environments in which most children live in Britain today. Examples of profiles drawn up by staffs in primary schools in a city centre and on a new housing estate illustrate the characteristics of particular locations.

School Environment Profile   A City Centre Primary School

This school of 340 children is situated in an established heavy industry area, near the city centre. The immediate vicinity could be classified as a socially deprived area, with its maze of brown-bricked terraced houses, broken only by the bustle of busy roads leading to the city centre. Much of this area is scheduled for slum clearance and re-development, but for various reasons the pace has been slow.

The school is bordered on the north by a densely populated area, and on the south by the docks and the railway line that serves them. To the west it is overshadowed by a large steel works, and to the east by light industries with some open park facilities.

This area lacks the normal social amenities of an urban community and consequently deprivation contributes to the breeding of petty crime which affects school children.

The buildings of the community are fairly recent — the oldest dating back to the second half of last century. The land was once marshy ground, but was subsequently drained and used to house the dock workers. The population is mixed and includes the descendants of Irish immigrants and other workers who moved south from the neighbouring industrial areas in search of work.

Unfortunately, these children rarely see rural or seaside features.

(a) *Features allowing for the development of locational skills* A variety of buildings exists in the school area, offering differences of design, construction material and function, e.g. houses, shops, hotels, factories, churches and chapels. However, at first glance this variety is not apparent because of the outward drabness and uniformity. Observations of traffic require careful supervision and to find an example of a contrasting rural environment would require a bus journey of at least five miles through busy streets. The only altitude variety is at least eight miles away and can only be viewed from the top of the nearby railway bridge.

The steelworks, light industries and docks provide study material for wider environments, but visits to these places are restricted to secondary pupils. However, some of the firms are prepared to allow their Public Relations Officers to give illustrated talks in schools. Similar use is made of some public services in the city — the fire brigade, postal services and the police.

(b) *Features allowing for the development of experimental and classificatory skills* The only obvious places where children could observe and classify plants are in two parks, situated approximately ten minutes' walking distance away. The variety of plants and flowers and trees is limited, and little collecting of specimens is possible.

The only other 'green areas' are those which lie on the very steep sides of the high railway cutting. For safety reasons it would be highly undesirable to encourage children to frequent these slopes.

Because of the large number of buildings it is impossible to observe rocks in their natural setting, such as on a quarry face or on a seashore cliff. Consequently, their collecting is limited to building stones strewn on roadsides and to materials from demolished buildings.

The study of living creatures in their natural state is confined to insects and birds; but a wide variety of domestic pets is available.

All the essential services exist, viz. water, electricity, gas and waste disposal. This allows an examination of the manufacturing process through its various stages.

(c) *Features allowing for the development of the concept of change* Old and˙ recent maps of the locality exist, together with an excellent collection of old photographs. The area has a local library, but the nearest museum is two miles away.

If the past changes of this locality are not altogether apparent, this is certainly not true of the present or the future. Today's and tomorrow's development plans are ever-present to these children who have to live in condemned property listening to demolition machines.

Change is, however, apparent in man's means of communication — from the school children see railways, roads and docks as well as aeroplanes in flight.

Implicit in any demolition work is social change. Recently demolished was an interesting row of houses named after the place of origin of the inhabitants who came to work in the steel works nearby.

A census of this area to show population/place of origin of the inhabitants shows that the society, although changing rapidly at present, has remained static for most of this century.

The absence of cultural and entertainment facilities in the community could provide a worthwhile starting-point for research into leisure-time habits and interests. One distinctive feature is the large number of chapels and churches.

School Environment Profile An Estate Primary School
The school, built in 1959, accommodates 500 junior school children. The building is situated 152 m above sea level in the centre of a post-war housing estate on what was once a boggy

and sparsely inhabited hill top. The population of the estate is 8,000 approximately and its area one square mile. However, the original estate is being rapidly encircled by a second phase of private residential development. On the outskirts of this mushrooming hilltop lies an old industrial township which contrasts dramatically with the immediate school environs.

The inhabitants of the original estate are of two types — people who have been re-housed following slum clearance in the city centre two miles away, and families who came from a distance of 100 miles or more in search of employment.

(a) *Features allowing for the development of locational skills*
At first glance the estate appears to be a series of uniform and colourless streets. A more deliberate examination, however, shows a variety of building types, e.g. multi-storey flats, terraced houses, bungalows, shops, post office, chapels, public houses. Although they do not display any striking differences, these buildings have been built from a variety of materials and in a variety of styles. Street patterns follow the relief — a hill top situation — but older ribbon development is within a few minutes' walk. The street names are interesting; the older ones are named after rivers, and the more recent are named like American avenues — First, Second, etc.

Sufficient through traffic exists to make census counts worthwhile. The exceedingly busy A48 which borders the estate provides a contrast in traffic flow and vehicle types. A new motorway, now under construction, will, however, alter the nature of the A48 at this point.

The view from the upper storey of the school must be one of the best for many miles — the sea to the south, the industrial complex of zinc works, oil refineries and steelworks, the mountains to the north and the lush countryside to the west. Unfortunately, all these require transport to make first-hand study possible. The course of the river, the main road and rail links can be followed for several miles. Examples of bridge types, viaducts, gradients and tunnels are either visible from the classroom or are within fifteen-minutes' walk.

A variety of factories in the neighbourhood will supply information to schools but will not allow visits from children under fifteen years of age. One other interesting building under construction on the fringe of the estate is a Ministry of Transport Tax Centre.

(b) *Features allowing for the development of experimental and classificatory skills*   Opportunities for collecting flora and fauna exist as the estate lies on the edge of the city and is bordered on one side by open ground and coal spoil heaps.

There is a good supply of flowers, plants and trees in this area, but wild life, except birds, is limited. The natural ponds of the area suffered in the initial estate development, so it is a rarity nowadays to have sticklebacks brought to the school. Limited weather records can be kept, but no weather recording apparatus can be left outside the school because of local vandalism.

The most fruitful study for the school would be the essential services as both a water tower and a service reservoir are situated outside the school gate, and an electric sub-station borders the playing fields. In the gardens of Clase House, next to the school, is the remains of a water fountain, which even twenty years ago was the main source of water for the neighbourhood. This could lead to a comparison of the present-day water supply with the past.

(c) *Features allowing for the development of the concept of change*   A famous old parish church stands within twenty minutes' walking distance from school. Its Celtic crosses, separate tower and the story of the annual fair once held in its grounds, never fail to arouse interest and provide fruitful starting-points for study. The estate is named after the monastery which used to be attached to this church. The inscriptions on the old grave stones show how children died at a very early age in the last century — evidence which invariably stimulates discussion and research into the living conditions of the past, diseases, medical services, surnames, etc.

The site is still the home for many elderly residents who remember bygone days in the parish. They can relate tales of transport to and from the city, food and travel prices, customs, what it was like farming and coalmining, rivalries and famous people of the district.

Other forms of 'living history' within the area are buildings such as the 'Smelter's Arms', established in 1766, with its links with the industrial past. Within twenty metres of this building is a post box with the letters 'V.R.' intact. On the other side of the estate lies the mother chapel of Welsh Nonconformity with the graves of eminent poets and musicians. Next door stands 'The Welcome' public house with its fine architecture. On one side of the school boundary wall stands Clase House, built in 1875, and designed by a famous architect who also built many chapels in the neighbouring town, all of which have similar architectural features. This house, together with three thatched roof cottages and a farm, now demolished, were the only dwellings marked on O.S. maps until as recently as 1948. These cottages once housed three tailor brothers, one of whom still lives on the estate.

Within fifteen minutes' walk of the school lie the ruins of the first flats built in Wales by Sir John Morris, founder of Morriston, to house his workers. Our school is a mile away from this town — maps of 1750 show its early planning on the 'grid' principle. The study of this contrasting environment lends itself to innumerable investigations.

This town is steeped in the history of copper, lead and tinplate manufacture and with coal mining. Derelict factories abound, and all of them can be traced from readily available sources, e.g. 1842 Tithe map, 1911, 1921, 1948, 1960 O.S. maps, together with various aerial photographs and documents. The canal, opened in 1800 to feed these industries, requires a slightly longer journey on foot. The social and economic ramifications of such a starting-point would more than balance the apparent paucity of concrete evidence near the school.

These profiles clarify some of the problems facing staffs in similar school areas. An appreciation of environmental studies by teachers has helped them to see their immediate areas as possible working places for the children. More varied locations provide more opportunities, but every environment contains usable material — and every school has its environment. Because some areas have greater potential than others is no reason for the often heard statement that 'there is nothing to study in our environment'.

In rural areas, movement outside the school is often easier than in towns, though even in the country safety precautions are essential for trips to rivers, cliffs and quarries and permission to visit private property cannot always be obtained. The following example of a rural school profile details the features likely to be found near many country schools. The variety of plant and animal life and the range of buildings provide material for a variety of studies, even though there are no opportunities for studying denser settled urban communities with their industrial and service provisions.

School Environment Profile   A Rural Primary School

This infant and junior mixed school of 68 children is situated in the lower reaches of a wide glaciated valley. The village itself, with its population of approximately 1,000, is bounded on the west by a mountain, rising to 531 m with steep limestone cliffs. To the east the mountainside sweeps down to a fertile sheltered valley ending in a wide river valley.

The parish, named after this village, was one of the original parishes of the county dating back to the Middle Ages; considerable boundary changes have been made since then, especially in the sixteenth and nineteenth centuries. The character and charm of the parish is reflected in the names of its farms — Ty Fry (Upper House), Ty Cwm (Dingle House) and Llwyn Celyn (The Holly Grove). They also indicate a mixture of high mountains, thickly wooded slopes and a rich, wide valley.

Although the village bears testimony to prehistoric man with its Neolithic burial chamber, its present elongated shape, and siting around the canal and stream, indicates that in the last century the canal was used for transporting lime from the quarries, and the stream for power to work the wool and flour mills. This rural community had its heyday with the coming of the canal in 1800, when the population was 1,000. By 1861 it had risen to 5,739.

(a) *Features allowing for the development of locational skills*
The village buildings belong mainly to the 1800–1860 or the 1950–1970 periods. Hardly any were built in the interval. Consequently, very little variety exists in these closely huddled river stone cottages, but recently a variety of new dwellings have mushroomed — council and private estates of detached and semi-detached houses and bungalows of different design and materials. Scattered within and around the village, are many old and beautiful dwellings and farmsteads — Elizabethan and Tudor houses, a

Welsh long house, and an old rectory which shows evidence of several additions and renovations dating back over five centuries. The parish church is basically Norman with Tudor additions. Although no great street variety exists, it would be possible to compare traffic flows on the main village road with the two branch roads. The village has two shops and a Post Office. The only employment within the village is in the building trade or agriculture. The people have to travel distances varying from 2 to 14 miles for their livelihood. Sheep, cattle, or mixed farming is still the main occupation, so land use studies can easily be undertaken.

A variety of altitude types surrounds the village and, in addition, suitable and convenient vantage points for study lie within five minutes' walk from the school. Again, old and new means of communication are within a stone's throw — tramroad, canal, river, stream, drover's road, turnpike road and toll gate, 'A' and 'B' roads, lanes and footpaths.

(b) *Features allowing for the development of experimental and classificatory skills*   The village is situated within a National Park area. The variety of the terrain — mountain, river, farmland, wood-land, bog and garden — offers limitless scope to develop the above skills. The land which lies within the 270 m and 450 m contour has been designated as a Nature Reserve, and contains rare trees, unusual plants, bird and animal life and extensive cave systems. Zoological, botanical, geological and comparative soil studies can all be made nearby.

The village now has a sewage scheme (1957), electricity (1938) and a water supply (1930). The many natural wells of the area, together with the recently installed North Sea Gas pipeline in the neighbouring village, could lead to a study of the essential services.

(c) *Features allowing for the development of the concept of change*   A range of features exist for the development of the above, e.g. a Neolithic burial ground, an Iron Age fort, a Norman church, a Norman castle, and a Roman road nearby, as well as the buildings already mentioned. Around each corner there is evidence of past occupation and customs — mounting blocks, blocked up windows, first floor barns, lime kilns, a pig sty at the rear of each house, a whipping stone and stocks, obsolete signposts, the overgrown graveyard of a now demolished chapel, drinking fountains, etc.

The most fruitful source of documentary evidence is the parish church where the parish register dating back to 1704, the birth, marriage and burial register, and the church rate book are kept. A variety of old and recent maps are available, e.g. 1842 Tithe map, O.S. maps for 1904 and 1967, geological and land use maps, aerial photographs (1947). Old photographs and other documents are in short supply. However, a visit to the County Library and Museum sixteen miles away would provide one with documents referring to Turnpike trusts and Drover's bank notes, besides stones, relics or other finds made in the area.

The County Water Board, Electricity Board and County Hall have proved to be useful sources of information for old maps, pipeline layouts, future development plans, etc. Because of the confidential nature of their information the Ministry of Agriculture refuse to divulge facts and figures relating to specific farms; the farmer himself is the best person for this.

When secondary and middle school staffs examine the potential of their environments, they should give greater consideration to the content but still emphasize the methods of working. The School Environment Profile by the staff members of a comprehensive school shows that, in addition to the skills, including sampling and mapping, there is also concern for particular tree studies, for the specific study of land use development and of environmental problems such as those associated with traffic and parking in the city.

School Environment Profile A City Comprehensive School

Description of the environment   The school used to be in the neighbouring city, a mile and a half away. In 1937 work was started on the present site in the grounds of a large manor house, but was halted during the war. It was opened in 1951. At that time it was one of the most modern and best equipped grammar schools in Wales.

It is situated in 'Parkland' and is virtually an extension of a large and beautiful public park, standing 54 m above sea level. To the south there is a panoramic view of an extensive bay from the top floor. The bay is situated within twenty minutes' walk of school. The average rainfall for the area is 1125 mm and the natural vegetation is woodland on the glacial soils covering the lower coal measures.

The school environment makes an interesting study as it is largely residential and much of the open space is purely recreational. No industries exist in the immediate neighbourhood. Transport is by road — no railways or canals exist at this end of the city.

Tithe maps are available for the area which give the basic road and field pattern for 1840.

The school is surrounded by a variety of large and interesting buildings like the old and new University College buildings, the hospital, the British Iron and Steel research buildings, shops centred around a very busy cross roads, and chapels and churches.

Possible lines of enquiry arising from the above environment

1 *Land use surveys*
   (a) Using the 1840 Tithe map as a base.
   (b) Development by 1900 — here the field work would be related to house types, the 1880 O.S. map being available.
   (c) Development by 1939 — the big addition would be the school itself together with the alteration of the busy crossroads nearby.
   (d) Changes by 1970 — the taking over of the Park Estate for Corporation housing development and the extensive building of private houses. This work would entail considerable mapping and field work.
   (e) One other aspect of this growth is the emergence of the adjoining village as a shopping centre. This could lead to suburban field work such as plotting and classifying shops on prepared Banda base maps. Their location could then be interpreted and shown by shading in on the 50 in. O.S. map of the whole area.

2 *Traffic census*
   There are now two major areas for this study:

(a) The crossroads with traffic lights and new restricted parking zones.
(b) The main road near the school. Safe stations for the conduct of observations of vehicle types and traffic flow exist.

3 *Weather studies*
Readings are taken at the school weather station and analyzed, though these are not available for the whole year.

4 *Field sketching*
The park, the streets and the bay.

5 *Contour mapping*
Within the park.

6 *Comparative studies*
The children have been corresponding with those in a Ghanaian secondary school.

There are opportunities for making comparisons between past and present conditions of the area because of the existence of old industrial sites and toll gates near the school.

Of great importance are the supplies of documentary evidence relating to the growth of the city. This material is available from the Royal Institute, the Borough Library and the extensive local historical resource packs, assembled through the local Teachers' Centre for use in schools. These collections of maps, documents and photographs provide extensive sources for the study of the development of transport, industry, trade and social conditions.

The fact that the school is situated within parkland does not allow for extensive 'natural habitat' studies. It is not surprising to see man's influence on the flora when one realizes that this parkland area was created by eminent industrialists. The neighbouring public park has a large variety of exotic trees. Beech and conifers have been planted to landscape the parklands — now overbuilt by the school, the University College, a large hospital and a residential estate. However, there are open public patches for study still remaining.

Below are some possible lines of enquiry that can be developed:

Study of a stream   Providing experiences in detailed ecology, flora and fauna, seasonal visits, etc.

Pond studies   Compare (a) chalet pond with (b) the boating lake.

Woodland surveys   Compare (a) a used woodland to the south of the school with (b) a woodland along the stream mentioned in *Study of a stream*. Both are good areas for ground cover plants and tree types (native and exotic).

The large public park
(a)   Completion of prepared base maps.
(b)   Stream study – within the park on a different site from above.
(c)   Dominant tree type – native, exotic, leaf collections, bark rubbings.
(d)   Special study of rhododendron garden.
(e)   Bird identification.

The seashore   Techniques involved are sampling, collecting, classifying, mapping, traversing, seasonal visits.

Examination of the area available for study is thus considered an important element in environmental studies organization in schools. Excursions on foot by staff members, the consultation of local large-scale maps, the seeking out of documentary and oral material for future use, all help to build up a resource central to their work in the school. As a first step, a headteacher with his staff can draw up an environment profile.

The School Estate
Schools and their estates vary enormously, but in every situation the environment of the school estate itself has to be considered as a resource for learning. The age, design and physical conditions of the school influence the provision of an attractive environment. Most modern school buildings include entrance halls, light airy corridors and rooms which provide space for plants and flowers, tanks of tropical fish, homes for hamsters, gerbils, stick insects and other living creatures, as well as exhibitions of children's art and other materials of interest.

Conditions in older schools where entrances are cramped and dingy, corridors gloomy and unattractive and space so limited that every corner has to be used for storage, make such display more difficult. Even in such conditions, however, many teachers have managed to bring beauty and interest into their working environment by turning convenient and gloomy places along corridors into attractive reading areas, making walls into display areas by the use of pinboard, and replacing extensive cloakroom areas by portable clothes stands.

No prescription can cover all the possible modifications as they depend upon the unique conditions in each school. It is necessary for the headteacher and staff to assess the conditions in which they and their children work. If the surroundings are bleak and colourless, lacking in interest, it is likely that an important element in the education of the children is being neglected.

The same attitude should be developed with regard to the school estate wherever possible. For some schools the estate consists of small asphalt strips, some of them on the roof, every square inch of which is required by the children during their breaks. The planting of trees and the development of bird feeding areas in such estates in unlikely to occur, but there are many schools where. concern for animal and plant life can take a practical form. The development of an experimental patch where flowers and vegetables are grown under various conditions can have an aesthetic as well as a scientific interest. The planting of a variety of trees and shrubs by the Local Authority or the P.T.A. is frequently encountered. There are often setbacks through vandalism, but even such acts as these can be turned to a good purpose by resourceful teachers.

An environmental studies section can be established in some new schools with an open area of ground. One school with a small stream running through the grounds has planned, with the participation of the children, to develop the area around the stream with various types of soil, rock outcrops, plants and nesting boxes. In another school an overgrown area has been cleared and turned into an attractive fish-pond and rockery by the top junior children. The activity itself was a good exercise in planning, including calculation of the volume of concrete needed and consideration of methods of water-proofing. And the result was an improvement in the school surroundings and the provision of features for environmental study (figs. 14–16).

Reference Books

Another resource needed by schools is a wide range of reference books for children and teachers. The ability to use reference books of increasing complexity is an essential skill for children. Without reference material available in the school, much of the environmental work will be limited and the children will be frustrated at not being able to follow up those aspects of study that have interested them. If books are not available, studies will rely only on local material, with the resultant dangers of parochialism. Books can in most instances be obtained from local libraries, but for many children the immediate availability of the right type of material is necessary to maintain interest and momentum. With limited financial resources, the building up of a satisfactory library will not be easy; but if a definite policy is undertaken, helped by long loans from county libraries, a fairly wide range of reference material can be collected.

The books obviously need to be attractive and well illustrated, and to cover a wide range of material in language suitable to the age of the children. Some books will concentrate on specific topics such as *Frogs*, or *Fire Engines* as in Methuens' *Stand and Stare* books, *Trees* and *Shells* as in Rupert Hart-Davis Educational's *Observe and Learn* series, or *The Chartists*, and *The Motor Revolution* as in Longman's *Then and There* series.

Other books confine themselves to suggesting how children may initiate studies themselves, as in Ginn's *Discovering your Environment* series, or Macmillan's *Discovery* books. Yet another type of reference book develops concepts such as classification, the use of keys and the identification of specimens by children. Attractive examples of this type are O.U.P.s *The Clue Books*, and Longman's *Town and Country* series.

Local Resource Material

Not all reference material, however, is to be found in books. Material showing the changing character of a local area can often be found in documents of various types and in maps and prints stored in archives, libraries and museums. As no concerted effort has as yet been possible for teachers, the material has not been available for use in schools.

With the growing awareness of the significance of the use of the locality in children's education a much greater provision of local material is being made by archivists, college departments, education advisory staff and teachers, sometimes working through Teachers' Centres.

In a number of areas, groups of teachers, in collaboration with their local archivist, librarian, or those with detailed knowledge of the locality, have produced packs of resource material for use in local schools. Most of this consists of reproductions of old maps, prints, photographs, broadsides and printed matter relating to local features. The groups, usually working through a Teachers' Centre but in some cases based on a school or college, have sifted the material available, and selected suitable items. These items have then been packaged, together with a handbook containing further information and suggestions, and made available to schools.

One area has concentrated on fairly broad themes such as transport and local industry; another has collected shoreline data; a third has provided documents illustrating bridges in the area; and yet another has outlined an industrial trail, backed by maps, prints and accounts of conditions in the eighteenth century. In all cases the concern has been to select a variety of sources from which children can extract information about an area easily accessible to them. Material exists for all areas but it requires positive action and the backing of the local education authority to make it available to the schools.

Some areas where documentation is sparse have been in particular difficulties. One way of solving this problem is to photograph significant features of the locality, write detailed accounts of each photograph, and then make sets of transparencies, prints and accounts available to local schools.

Inevitably schools have developed their own sets of documentary evidence. In some schools resource centres have been established where, in addition to the documentary material, samples of clothing, tools, domestic utensils and other articles from the past have been collected. These form working museums for the schools (fig. 13).

There is no single way in which material related to the locality can be gathered; but unless such material is made available, some stunting of an environmental studies approach is inevitable. More nationally significant material has been and will be produced commercially, but the detailed local material can only be produced locally — and teachers must play their part in this activity.

Equipment and Apparatus

There is little equipment or apparatus required for an environmental studies approach that is not already found in a reasonably equipped school. Measuring equipment of various types, safe sources of heat and water, together with a range of simple scientific equipment should be available. Children should be encouraged to make their own apparatus so that what is needed is an extensive range of wires, bulbs, glass rods, nails, screws and such like, rather than specialized pieces of equipment. One basic piece of equipment that many schools lack is a large scale map of the school area. Provision of 50 in. or 25 in. maps of the area, together with 6 in., $2\frac{1}{2}$ in. and possibly 1 in. maps are an essential requirement. Some audio-visual equipment is very useful in work of this kind, though it should not be considered indispensable. A slide projector is of great value, not only to illustrate local features, but also for use by children when making large scale illustrations of the locality. A slide of a building or activity when projected onto a large sheet of paper can be outlined accurately and later coloured. The quality of the resulting illustration is a source of pride and achievement and encourages children to undertake artistic activities.

The use of a portable tape recorder is also of great value. The taping of sounds or impressions in the field, the recording of interviews and the recording of a written script to accompany a set of slides all give pleasure and experience to the children. As children hear themselves on tape they begin to show interest in their speech and expressions.

Cine projectors, cameras, television sets, radios, microprojectors, tumbler polishing machines and other apparatus can add to the quality of the work, but should not be considered essential equipment. In some schools, the use of photography requires cameras, a dark room, developing and printing equipment — all of value in particular circumstances.

Transport

One final resource needed by schools is some form of transport. For many schools long journeys are not necessary for environmental studies, but in others they are of considerable importance. All schools will sometimes require a long journey to follow up a theme or to make a contrast with the locality.

Such transport is provided in a variety of ways. More and more local authorities are providing funds for transport of junior and middle school children as well as those at secondary level. Individual schools use their school funds, make a charge on the children, or in some cases organize transport in parents' cars. There is no single form of provision — it depends on the ingenuity of headteacher and staff.

In some schools the problem has been solved by the purchase of a motor-bus or mini-bus. A small school in Shropshire is a fine example of the initiative of the staff, parents and children who collected money and bought their own mini-bus. The question of transport, as with so much else, depends on the school. If the headteacher and staff consider that the visit is really in the interests of the children, a means of providing for it will be found — if not, it will not.

3 The Skills of Environmental Studies

The environment of a school can provide a rich source of study, especially when its potential has been assessed by headteacher and staff and complemented by provision of suitable secondary resource material. This will help to set up a normal condition for working in the school, unaffected by staff changes or the fact that many teachers themselves live outside the local school environment.

Even if these provisions have been made, the way in which the resources are used will depend upon the understanding by the school staff of the significance for children of the curriculum field involved. Gifted teachers have for long used the environment as a stimulus for creative and analytical work, but experience has shown that such activities, though numerous, are generally isolated. In a small rural school the influence of a teacher in this field may be of great significance to children throughout their lives, but in the majority of large schools where such activities have been infrequent they have generally left little lasting impression.

The value of environmental studies has already been stated in some detail. It is now necessary to consider more carefully ways of implementing such work in a wide variety of schools.

Topics

Early attempts to bring some pattern to environmental studies were based upon a selection of topics. These topics were generally features of the locality which could be subjected to direct first-hand investigation in the field, thereby involving children in studies of their physical and social environments.

An example of such an approach is given by the following table of some topics studied over a four-year period in a junior school of 250+ children in a large village. It is a school where considerable thought and preparation has been given to the work throughout the school so that it can well serve as an illustration of good practice in this curriculum field.

The titles of the topics illustrate the growth in complexity. From a study based on 'My House' when the children enter the school, they move to other sites in the locality until they study the village and its connections with the outside world before they leave school. The topics studied by one class over four years can be followed with greater precision by reading diagonally from top left to bottom right in the table of topics shown above.

Topics studied in a Junior School

	7–8 years	8–9 years	9–10 years	10–11 years
ar 1	My house People we meet in the street The school and its situation	The shop window The castle and abbey Hobbies	Roads leading from village A coastal transect A farming study	Roads leading from village Norman castle and modern house Growth of our village
ar 2	My house People we meet in the street My school	Food, water, air Visit to local church Other communities in our village	Roads to and from village The local lake Farming	The town hall A village survey The story of flight
ar 3	My house People we meet in the street The school and its situation	Shops Castle, abbey and priory Pets	Roads leading from village The river valley The school area	The local lake Parish boundaries A village survey
ar 4	My house People we meet in the street Our school	Shops Castle, abbey and priory Hobbies	Roads leading from village Coastal transect Farming	The local lake The local lake Our village

1st year	2nd year	3rd year	4th year
My house People we meet in the street The school and its situation	Food, water and air A visit to the local church Other communities in our village	Roads leading from village The river valley The school area	The local lake The local lake Our village

There is an attempt to develop a scheme with a strong element of concentricity built into it in many though not in all schools. This reflects children's growing awareness of the immediate world and its expanding horizons, though little study beyond the limits of the village is required by the titles. In practice, however, features such as the local lake and village roads, provide opportunities for children to deal with much wider horizons in space and time.

The growth in complexity is not evident throughout the scheme, for while studies generally change from single-site topics to more complicated, larger and varied areas, there are some topics such as 'The Story of Flight'. 'Pets', 'Food', 'Water and Air', which do not fit easily into this pattern (see p. 51). They may be undertaken on a direct enquiry basis, but are of a different nature from the other starting-points.

Another feature which interrupts the overall framework is the repetition of particular starting-points in successive years. The local lake is studied with the nine to ten-year-olds but it appears again the following year. The studies may have been undertaken at different levels, but repetition of this type may limit the range of interests children could have followed.

In spite of these anomalies the general scheme followed in this particular school did have an element of continuity providing for the increasing growth of awareness but allowing for the interests of children to influence the topics studied. In many schools such a general pattern is lacking. Starting-points arrived at by a variety of means are haphazard and of limited depth, and they give little attention to increasing complexity or extension.

The titles of topics, however, give little indication of the work actually developed by children. A clearer view can be gained by considering the methods that were used. This information, gained through direct contact with the school together with an analysis of the teachers' detailed accounts, is summarized in the chart opposite (top). The lists shown for each year represent the activities undertaken by the children within the class. The order in which they appear in the lists has no significance except for clarity.

A study of the activities shows that certain features, e.g. discussions, mapping, experimenting and imaginative writing occurred in each of the four years. Other activities such as the

Study methods used in school topics

	My House People we meet in the Street The School and its Situation *1st year. 7–8-year-olds*	Food, Water and Air Visit to Local Church Other Communities in the Village *2nd year. 8–9-year-olds*	Roads leading from Village The River Valley The School Area *3rd year. 9–10-year-olds*	The Local Lake Our Village *4th year. 10–11-year-olds*
1	Discussing	Discussing	Discussing	Discussing
2	Experimenting	Experimenting	Experimenting	Experimenting
3	Factual written records	Factual written records	Factual written records	Factual written records
4	Use of tape recorder	Use of tape recorder	Use of tape recorder	Use of tape recorder
5	Mapping	Mapping	Mapping	Mapping
6	Imaginative writing	Imaginative writing	Imaginative writing	Imaginative writing
7	Collecting	Collecting and classifying	Use of reference books	Use of reference books
8		Use of reference books	Mathematics	Mathematics
9		Mathematics		Mounting and displaying
10		Mounting and displaying		Letter writing
11		Letter writing		Modelling
12				

Study methods reflecting teacher interests

	The School Road *1st year. 7–8-year-olds*	The Park *2nd year. 8–9-year-olds*	The Stream *3rd year. 9–10-year-olds*	The Shopping Centre *4th year. 10–11-year-olds*
1	Use of reference books	Use of reference books	Use of reference books	Use of reference books
2	Class discussions	Class discussions	Class discussions	Class discussions
3	Written records (factual)	Written records (factual)	Written records (factual)	Written records (factual)
4	Collecting and classifying	Collecting and classifying	Collecting and classifying	
5	Mounting and displaying	Mounting and displaying	Mounting and displaying	
6	Modelling	Modelling		
7	Pictorial representation			
8	Plans and maps			
9			Experimenting	
10			Mathematics	

use of reference books and mathematics occurred with only three classes. Collecting, and classifying, mounting and displaying, modelling and letter-writing occurred in only one or two of the years. This pattern suggests that although certain skills were called upon at all stages of development, others occurred spasmodically or infrequently. If this is the situation in a school where considerable thought and planning has led to a wide repertoire of study methods, the situation in schools where less planning has taken place is much less satisfactory.

The lower chart (p. 53) sets out the activities undertaken by children over a period of four years in a city school. Here the difference between the years is more obvious. Many very significant activities are confined to one of the four years only, and the fourth year strikingly confines itself to writing and discussions. This is a common feature of schools where the range of activities is limited and largely depends on the teacher, or where hardly any consultation between classes occurs.

One of the prime causes for this variation in the range of skills is the fact that many children are engaged on studies to see *what* they can find out about a particular feature of the environment. But the emphasis should be on *how* to study the environment. If information is the objective of the study, then reference books and an ability to read and write will suffice. In a large school where a child has a number of different teachers over the years, the skills used at any particular stage will depend upon the views of the individual teachers unless there is some agreed policy for the school.

The approach to a study of the environment on the basis of topics chosen within individual classes without reference to a school policy, therefore, has serious disadvantages. Though individual teachers can produce stimulating and purposeful work using a wide range of methods, environmental studies needs to be looked at in the school rather than the classroom context. Some schools have moved a long way towards providing a substantial framework within which teachers can function freely but even then the range of study methods may be ragged and uncertain. Many teachers may wish to adopt this approach but before doing so they should consider the advantages of an alternative one based upon the skills involved in such studies.

An Approach through Skills

The nature of these skills has already been discussed. Teachers have become more conscious of their value and the opportunity they provide for a pattern which avoids the chaos that can arise through unorganized investigation. With greater experience many schools now recognize the value in co-ordination of work between classes through a specification of the skills involved. Those making a potentiality profile of an area must be clear in their minds what skills are to be developed, and encourage the children to choose those features that would provide opportunities for the involvement of a wide range of skills.

In this lies the essential difference between the two methods of using the environment. In the first, an interesting feature is chosen and examined for its intrinsic interest and information. In the second method the environmental features are regarded as raw materials through the examination of which children develop a wide range of skills and understandings. The particular use of the environment will vary with the age and ability of the children concerned and only the teacher can decide the relevance of particular skills to a child.

For children in the infant school the environment involves all experiences both in and out of school. In fact teaching today emphasizes the importance of making available a wide range of. objects and practical experiences, including a variety of colours, shapes and textures, living and growing animals, suitable tools of various kinds, and a range of colourful and attractive books and posters. These, together with radio, television, tape recorders and projectors are considered necessary resources. The provision of an interesting school environment, often to combat the squalor and dullness of the home and locality, is fairly typical of many infant schools today.

'Yesterday we went down to the stream to let our tadpoles and newts go in freedom. Mrs. Foster got on a pease of wood and emptied them out again. Then we played and the cows were in the water under the bridge and then we went back home to school and sat under the oak tree to have a cool rest, and then Ante Mary came by with baby Jane and David and we found that we had missed one newt.'

Often the extent of the environment used is wider than that

of the immediate school estate. Unable to alter the environment physically, teachers select particular features which they consider will interest and stimulate their children.

In some infant schools large-scale models of the locality have been made by the combined efforts of children, teachers and parents. Children, sometimes using work cards, examine the models, trace out routes on them, make simple maps, describe some features — generally use them for developing ways of recording and communicating.

'Before the study of the river made by this class of six to seven year olds, a large model of the district had been made. One of the main features of this model was the river. Alongside the model was a large number of work cards devised and produced by the teacher, so that the children could use it in a practical manner. These work cards gave them experience in relating the positions of buildings to their school and home, practice in reading, measuring and writing simple descriptions.'

Lower Junior Children
Diagram 1 illustrates the objectives of an environmental studies approach with upper infant and lower junior children. Three groups of skills are shown with the major emphasis given to aspects of the basic and social skills. The reason for this is the importance of the basic skills, especially language, as a pre-requisite for more detailed environmental studies at a later stage.

To read with understanding and pleasure is one of the main objectives for a primary school child and until this has been achieved, the development of other skills will be limited. An examination of the locality of the school in Diagram 1 showed a number of possible starting-points within a short distance of the school. Occupations existing in a street, the variation within a park, the building materials used locally, and the growth of the area itself, all include many facets for providing varied studies. Other starting-points could be suggested by children or teachers.

A teacher will have to consider the possible activities in which the children can become involved and the tools and techniques they may require. An example of such anticipation is given in the following suggestions for work based on 'The Street of Shops'.

Diagram 1　Some Skills Related to Infant/Junior Studies

	Skills	Objectives	Possible Starting-points
	Basic		
1	Using reference books	To indicate the nature, purpose and use of simple reference books	The street of shops
2	Questionnaires	To compile simple questions for the gathering of required information	How our estate began
3	Factual writing	To report factual information accurately	The materials needed to build our school
4	Imaginative writing	To encourage personal expression based upon first-hand experiences	Our homes
5	Mathematics	To make some aspects of mathematics more meaningful through practical experiences	The park
6	Modelling and pictorial representation	To extend a child's imaginative powers by an introduction to a range of media	Occupations in Church Street
	Social Skills and Attitudes		
7	Conduct of class discussions	To assist a child to develop fluency, confidence and tolerance	
8	Respect for the environment	To develop a concern for people and features within the environment	
	Study Skills		
9	Use of maps and plans	To develop the ability to use maps and plans to study and represent an area	
10	Collecting and classifying	To classify living and non-living things in various ways	
11	Experimenting	To design and undertake tests and interpret results	

The Street of Shops Topic for Infants/Lower Juniors
An illustration of some of the skills that might be practised by children in the study of the suggested topic and the aspects related to the skills.

1 *Using Reference Books*
Information on commodities; towns/countries of origin; shops long ago; commodities long ago.

2 *Imaginative Writing*
Journey of a commodity; adventures of any item bought from a shop; creating advertising posters. Foods and other items in the future.

3 *Factual Writing*
'The visit to the shops'; a description of a chosen shop; how I took the photographs.

4 *Mapping*
Route from home to shops; route of commodity from source to shop, etc.

5 *Modelling and Pictorial Representation*
Models of types of ships (oil tanker, refrigerated, etc.); frieze of shops.

6 *Collecting and Classifying*
Types of commodities; statistics on popular shopping hours (census); registration numbers on cars of shoppers; types of shops.

7 *Mathematics*
Graphs of statistics gathered; practical shopping exercises.

8 *Questionnaires*
Construction suitable for shopkeepers and/or shoppers.

9 *Discussions*
How can we study the shops? Claims of advertizers for their products; results of statistics gathered, interpretation.

Instead of emphasizing only language and pictorial representation, other activities are specified by the teacher. 'The street of shops' will be subjected to study by a wide variety of methods, each requiring its particular skills and equipment. If the language level of the children is low, the concentration may be on the writing and speech activities. But there are opportunities also for practical exercises on money used in shopping, and frieze, collage and model work based on the theme of shops and commodities may also be undertaken.

Within this context of traditional skills, specific activities involving simple plan- and map-making, grouping data and experimenting can be introduced. Different methods of collecting data will be used, tests on different commodities conducted, and the results recorded and grouped in a variety of ways. There will not be a high level of competence but the children will be learning the analytical processes – observing closely, recording accurately and questioning the evidence they have gathered.

The Middle Years of School
The framework of skills for environmental studies with older children in junior, middle and lower secondary schools is shown by Diagram 2 (see p. 60).

Compared with the earlier situation the priority of the children's activities has altered on the assumption that they have reached a reasonable degree of literacy, and the core of the work now is the further development of the study skills. Children in this age range are capable of reading and constructing maps containing all the basic requirements of recording and communication. Further developments of the experimental method, of posing questions, formulating hypotheses and devising experiments form another line of progression leading to a scientific attitude in children. This can be strengthened by using a more precise and varied classificatory system. Younger children grouped materials on the basis of one common characteristic. Now, multiple criteria and the use of keys should become part of the equipment of investigatory techniques. With the increasing availability of photographs and documents of a local, regional and national nature, more attention needs to be paid to the interpretation of these sources for an understanding of the various methods of representing reality.

Involvement in the environment assists the growth of social conduct and language gives form to the studies. These are constant features of the approach at all levels, though their significance varies at different stages. Diagram 3 (see pp. 62–3) outlines the planning that goes into an undertaking of a transect study with a class. The five groups involved will each be dealing

Diagram 2 Some Skills Related to Junior/Lower Secondary Studies

Skills	Objectives	Possible Starting-points
Study		
1 Mapping	The use and understanding of suitable mapping techniques for studying an area	A transect through the valley
2 Collecting and classifying	To develop classificatory skills including the construction and use of identification keys	The local stream
3 Experimenting	To practise design, observation, recording and interpretation when conducting experiments under control	An old church
4 Construction and use of questionnaires	The construction and use of questionnaires though recognizing the privacy of the individual	Our water supply
5 Use of documents and old photographs	To further an awareness of past conditions and future possibilities through the use of these media	Boundaries, paths and roads
Basic		
6 Using reference books	To give the children an opportunity to compare reference books of various types	
7 Factual writing	To develop a concise and accurate style of reporting factual information	
8 Imaginative expression	Personal expression in a variety of media based upon first-hand experiences	
9 Mathematics	To make some aspects of mathematics more meaningful by practical application	
10 Modelling	Use of a variety of media with a recognition of scale	
Social Skills and Attitudes		
11 Conduct of class and group discussions	To assist a child to develop his power of oral discussion, to form and express opinions and to respect the opinions of others	
12 Respect for environment	The development of attitudes of respect and concern for the quality of the environments in which we live	

with different aspects within the total study, but they can all be involved in similar skills though based upon varied situations. For example, rocks, plants, animals, buildings and vehicle registration numbers may have been collected by different methods but the classifying and identifying processes are similar. The quarry, reservoir, canal, road and buildings all need maps of different types, and all raise questions on the physical nature of such features as soil, water, oxygen, traffic lights and sash windows.

As with all other skills, children will show different rates of progress. No precise ceiling of achievement can or should be specified, though considerable guidance as to expectation is already available, such as the Bristol Achievement Tests in Study Skills.

The Small Primary School

Problems of the different rates of progress are magnified in small primary schools where one class may include children of a wide range of ages and abilities. Many cases exist of children aged between seven and eleven years being taught in the same class, a situation requiring a particularly sensitive approach by the teacher. In small schools the skills developed by the individual children must be the teacher's main concern. Different groupings of children may be used within the class, but whatever system is employed, careful attention has to be paid to the type of work each child undertakes.

Seven-year-olds in contact with their eleven-year-old class-mates may well be motivated to draw maps, make careful exhibitions and test materials, but their performances will normally be inferior to those of their more experienced friends. Manual dexterity, their stage of mental development and their level of competence in the basic skills will make their studies different in level and nature from those of the older children.

A teacher in this situation has, within the one class, to vary the purpose of environmental studies for the individual child. The younger children, though involved in the class or group study, should have their main attention directed to activities involving language. They may make collections, examine photographs, ask questions and draw simple maps, but the teacher will use each activity chiefly as a means of language development through descriptions of collections, annotations of photographs, posing questions in different ways in questionnaires, and explaining how the maps were drawn.

Diagram 3   Possible Activities in a Transect across a Val

	Stone Quarries	A Reservoir
Collecting and classifying	Rocks Rock plants	
Experimenting	Soil and rock tests	How is water cleaned? What is a syphon?
Mathematics		Volume, area
Mapping exercises	Dating quarries by OS maps	Catchment area
	Symbols	Area supplied
Comparison of past, present and future	Stone mason – a dying trade	Ancient wells, artesian t
Modelling	Quarry face showing strata	A reservoir system, e.g. Fechan
Questionnaires	Interviewing elderly folk	Interviewing staff
Use of reference books	Identifying specimens	Varied aspects
Old documents, photographs	Quarry eighty years ago	Report of 1906 taken fr The Quarry

The older children in the class or group concentrate more on the development of their study skills. Their increasing competence in scientific investigation, their greater ability in the use of maps, graphs and other diagrammatic forms of representation provide objectives for their younger colleagues with whom they are working.

Diagram 4 (see p. 64) is an analysis of the study based on a village area undertaken by twenty-five children aged seven to eleven years in the junior section of a two-teacher rural school.

Disused Canal	Streets and Buildings	A Main Road
ants and pond life una along canal	Types of buildings – use Types of buildings – age	Vehicle numbers Road classification
xygenating plants	How do 'sash-windows' work?	How do traffic lights work?
rgo costs based on tolls	Graphs of houses per street Graphs of number of occu- pants – census	Census of traffic types Census of density flow
ute of canal nals of other countries	Land use maps showing function and age	Main routes of county Main routes of country
rges, cargoes mpetition with railway	Development of use of materials for building	Transport the road has seen People who use and have used the road Types of road
ock barge	Development of dwellings Sectional model of modern house	Cross-section of modern Roman road
terviewing elderly folk	Interviewing elderly folk	Interviewing passers-by
formation on world canals, ilders, etc.	Varied aspects of materials	Information on road building major world routes
d canal photographs	Old photograph of streets MOH report on housing, 19th century	Posters, broadsides, old Commission Reports

These children were accustomed to working in groups which
were not rigid units, but varied with the particular requirements of
the situation, and the individual children. Five aspects of the village
area were studied – the hill on which most buildings were located,
the buildings themselves, the inhabitants the river at the base of
the hill and the bridge which crossed the river.

As the diagram on this page illustrates, the activities involved
could be used at different levels. For example, plans of buildings,
large-scale plans of the village street and smaller-scale maps of the

Diagram 4   The Village Area
A Study by 7–11-year-old pupils in a Rural Area

Study Skills

Experimentation	Maps and Plans	Comparison
Construction of level indicator clinometer	Plan of village 'street'	Roads through ages
Breaking strain	Old drovers' road	Village long ago
Effect of weedkillers	Modern roads	
Effect of fertilizers	Source of local river	Use of tithe map – old names
	Buildings	
	School catchment area	

Basic Skills

Mathematics	Reference Books	Modelling
Census of traffic – nearby main road	Famous road builders	Village area
Graphs of types of buildings, heights	Origins of road materials	Types of bridges, buildings
Surveying old chapel site	Famous bridge builders	Old village crafts
Census of population – graphs		
Use of clinometer		
Speed of river		

Social Skills

Attitudes
Constructing questionnaires and interviewing people
Conservation of local features

national road system, were all involved in the study, thus providing for a wide spread of ability and understanding of maps within the class. Similarly, the mathematical and classificatory activities ranged from simple histograms of building types to flow graph of traffic.

In addition to these activities a great deal of creative writing on the river was forthcoming as well as pictorial representation of a variety of aspects. Local inhabitants were interviewed and in some instances valuable information on the story of the hamlet was tape-recorded.

Children from Eleven to Thirteen Years

Children in the lower forms of secondary schools or the upper section of middle schools also concentrate upon study skills in their environmental studies, though other elements begin to take on greater significance at this stage as children reach a higher level of competence in analysing their physical and social context. These elements include the role of people in environmental change, greater recognition of environmental problems such as pollution, and the impending, more specialized, subject-divided curriculum that many of the children will be following.

Involvement in a study of children's environments can lead to positive actions like beautifying the area or providing some social amenity that is lacking. In some new schools, children have participated in the planning of part of the school estate; in others unattractive sections of the school grounds have been turned into rockeries, flower gardens and fishponds. In all such projects the teacher must plan the activity so that it involves a wide range of skills and resources. The small-scale change in the children's environment is seen as a personal illustration that environments can be altered by conscious acts.

Outside the school estates both theoretical and practical changes in the environment have played a part in the studies developed. A class of eleven-year-old children studied a local road junction where traffic jams were a considerable problem. They decided a fly-over was the only way to alleviate the difficulty. When it was realized that the construction of the fly-over would lead to the destruction of many houses, including some of their own, the social problems involved in change became a personal matter. A similar reaction resulted where children in studying water supply examined the ideal conditions for reservoir construction. As the teacher reports:

'I asked them if they were given the job to look for a new site for a reservoir could they think of one place that contained all the points that they had listed — and I ran through them again, giving them time to think. It suddenly dawned on them that their valley, where they themselves lived, would make a very good place to build a reservoir. At once, there was uproar and objections raised.'

The idea of possible change in their localities has developed into positive acts where children have helped by tree-planting to cover old waste heaps, and to rescue and restore old industrial sites of archaeological value. They have provided information boards on local features or simply helped in clearing refuse and litter. All such activities represent the increasing involvement in the quality of the environment that can arise through studies of this type. It is such an attitude that is necessary to ensure that future environments are of as high a quality as possible.

The Bridge to Subjects

For many children the change from a broad approach of environmental studies to the more fragmented view of subjects may not be to their advantage. For these a continuation of a more integrated approach may be adopted during their secondary school lives. Others, however, benefit from following a more specialized subject-divided pattern.

If such divisions are to occur, it will be advantageous to recognize them in the later stages of environmental studies work in primary schools. Basically, the children will be changing from an approach requiring a specified list of skills to a group of subjects each with its particular method and body of knowledge. Up to this stage, children will have been encouraged to follow their interests in learning how to study and represent a wide range of material; but from this point they will learn how to use their study skills in depth in relationship to specified material much of which will be represented in diagrammatic, statistical, pictorial or cartographical form.

The selection of features to be visited will probably be linked more precisely to the general requirements of the subjects. For example, a transect across a valley undertaken by a class of twelve to thirteen-year-olds was chosen to bring out the variations in land use and emphasize the existence of areas of difficulty. This geographical concept was then developed by the teacher on a broader scale by detailed examination of other major

areas of difficulty. The local study was here used as an e.
of a feature with world-wide implications. Within the same transect
locations were chosen for detailed examination of soil and plant
characteristics to bring out the inter-related features involved in an
ecological system. Previous experience in direct investigation by
the children was given a more specific component by a theoretical
statement of the method required by scientific examination of
field features. In such various ways a bridge should be provided
to the more abstract, formalized subject studies children will meet
in their secondary schools.

Summary

Environmental studies is considered to provide a progressive
approach for use with a wide range of children.

At infant school, the children themselves, their families,
friends and home provide stimuli for basic skills and the first
steps in some simple study skills and scientific attitudes.

Later, as they develop to a stage where language can be used
reaonably fluently, the environment is considered a vehicle for the
development of study skills of increasing complexity and accuracy.

Still later, with further expertise, some children can take a more
analytical view of the environment which prepares them for a
study of specialist subjects, though for others a more integrated
approach will be of greater value.

Through such a process children will expand their range of
skills and concepts, increase their facility in language, number and
creative arts and develop a greater awareness of themselves and
the place and society in which they exist, as well as a concern
for the maintenance and development of their future environments.

The nature and value of an environmental studies approach and the organizational steps needed for its functioning have already been dealt with. This chapter examines the main problems of the approach at the working-face level. The suggestions are the result of observations and discussions in a variety of schools, examination of written reports from teachers and experiences gained in meetings and courses. More detailed illustrations are provided by *Case Studies*, a companion volume to this book.

Many of the suggestions here may seem obvious to teachers experienced in this type of work. But for a teacher who has been used to a precise time-table with a specified factual syllabus, working within one classroom, it may be unnerving to face an investigation of the outside world, with no precise objectives. Unless this aspect is appreciated and appropriate steps taken, the experience can sap the confidence of a teacher and so diminish the value of the whole activity.

'Through lack of experience, I agreed with the children that they should study all their lines of interest. This meant thirty-six different topics! It was not long, however, before I realized that the scope of the work was far too wide and varied and 'that I was quite unable to help all the children, to keep a check on the work produced, nor provide sufficient reference material for everyone's needs.'

The teacher who wrote this could well have retreated into his original teaching situation after the disappointment of this venture. Fortunately, he had the support of a sympathetic head-master and realized that organization, control and provision of resources are essential before an environmental studies approach can be used. He can now cope with the problems of a large number of individual topics.

Whether teachers plunge into the problems and work out the answers, or whether they are cautious in their approach will depend on personalities. Here we examine the practical problems.

The School Approach

If a teacher is working as part of a school programme, discussions between headteacher and staff are necessary. In small primary schools there is no problem as staff members are few and the headteacher is aware of the progress of all the children.

Large schools do, however, have particular problems. Informal discussions take place but these do not appear to be particularly effective. Formal discussions in staff meetings have proved necessary in many schools, especially when first introducing the approach. In some of the larger schools, headteachers have appointed a curriculum development teacher either to deal with the problems over the school as a whole or within each year group.

Whatever method is employed, a teacher needs to be aware of the aims and objectives of the work and how his particular class relates to the school strategy. Wider contacts with other schools through visits, use of the Teachers' Centre, and discussions with advisory and college staffs, can also help to decrease the isolation of individual teachers.

Another factor to be considered is informing parents of the nature of the work. Parents who have had little or no experience of learning through direct investigation will be unable to understand the purpose of the activities. In many schools, slide-and-tape accounts of studies have been shown to the parents concerned, or headteachers and others have given illustrated talks to inform parents of the purpose and nature of the work.

Degree of Control

A general problem facing many teachers is the amount of direction or control they should exercise over the work of the children. Extreme approaches are rare, as the degree of control necessary varies with the age and ability ranges of the children, and the experience and ability of the teacher. The role of the teacher is evolutionary in nature, gradually providing a freer condition for study but never completely abdicating.

When a teacher new to this approach encounters a class accustomed to a formal mode of instruction, a considerable degree of direction and control is necessary. A starting-point close to the school will probably be chosen to which short, tightly disciplined visits will be made. Assignments on the visit will be specified, but opportunities for individual interests provided. There will probably be a specific allocation of time, usually two afternoons, or three to four hours a week, over a fairly short time, e.g. six weeks.

A more experienced teacher dealing with children inexperi-

enced in the approach will be able to modify such a strictly-controlled pattern, but there will still be a considerable amount of direction. The site for study may offer a greater variety of interests for which suitable reference material is available. Class teaching will play a less significant role in favour of greater use of group and individual studies. Occasionally an inexperienced teacher is confronted by a class mature in their approach. In such a situation discussions with the headteacher and colleagues are invaluable.

When both children and teacher are experienced, a co-operative relationship leading to enquiry and discovery is possible. There is no rigid time-table and children participate in the planning, organization and conduct of the studies. A wide range of resources allows for a variety of lines of enquiry; children know how to conduct and organize group and individual studies in the field and; with the help of the teacher, record, experiment and display within the classroom. But the teacher must still be in charge.

A striking feature of environmental studies is the change it brings about in teachers. For many, the introduction of this approach has brought new interests to their lives. Often starting tentatively and lacking confidence they have gradually become aware of the possibilities of study around them, looking at their surroundings with a more perceptive and analytical eye. As one teacher said, 'If you told me three years ago that I would spend a Saturday afternoon searching on gravestones to find evidence of past professions in this area, I would have thought you were mad!'

The degree of control expected from a teacher cannot be prescribed as only the teacher knows the requirements of his class. He must, however, accept that an environmental studies approach requires that his role evolves as changes take place within himself and his children.

Time Allocation
One feature reflecting the growth in the experience of teachers is the amount of time given to environmental studies. Infant schools rarely have a rigid time-table, though in many junior schools the use of particular facilities such as television, the school hall or the field make some time-table necessary. However, arrangements are flexible and blocks of time are specified for particular activities.

When first starting environmental studies, most teachers have found a limited commitment to the approach advisable, and have used the time previously specified for such items as geography, history, science, centres of interest or local studies. This has generally meant three to four hours or two afternoons per week, though the time varies greatly at secondary level.

With increasing experience and growing confidence this deliberate limiting of time and material is modified, especially at junior school level. Children's desires to express their discoveries or sensations in a variety of ways break down the boundaries. Therefore teachers find it increasingly difficult to specify how much time every week should be taken from other curriculum fields and given to environmental studies. It should be emphasized that this does not mean that the whole curriculum is covered through this approach, but that other skills developed by different approaches are used and improved when the occasion demands.

Frequently, records kept by individual teachers show the following progression in time allocation for environmental studies.

Year 1. Time allocation four hours/week during geography, history and science time.

Year 2. Time allocation, time-table flexible — overflow into basics, at least five to six hours/week.

Year 3. Time allocation difficult to say — has varied from forty minutes to sixteen hours/week on this topic.

The blocking of time-tables has proved useful in lower secondary school forms. In one school a co-operative teaching system worked successfully: 'Each class has eight periods of thirty-five minutes of environmental studies per week and each specialist teacher has the same amount. The time-table is arranged in blocks so that all the pupils (four classes of approximately thirty-two pupils in each) and staff are involved at the same time and interchanges and visits can take place.'

Length of Studies
An examination of studies undertaken by a number of teachers has shown a great variation in the period over which they have been maintained. There are instances of particular studies continuing for two terms; on the other hand, topics have failed

after two or three weeks owing to lack of interest by the children and inadequate preparation by the teacher. The evidence available suggests that for younger junior children a period of five to six weeks is sufficient to satisfy their interests whereas with older children eight to ten weeks is the optimum. Considerably longer studies have been recorded but these studies, though nominally based upon one starting-point, have diverged so widely that the later points are only tenuously related to the earlier work. For example, a study which commenced on a stream led to land use, the life history of the nearby houses, past and present use of the roads over the stream, a wide series of experiments on the conditions for plant growth and the clearing of the stream section in the school grounds to make a flower garden. Maintenance of the children's interest is the main factor controlling the length of a study. If attempts to stimulate or re-channel interests fail, the study should be rounded off rather than dropped. The need to complete a task undertaken is a requirement of such investigatory work.

Visits
Local as well as more distant visits form an essential part of environmental studies (fig. 7). The local authority regulations regarding teacher—pupil ratios on excursions should be consulted so that the legal position is clarified. There is no national uniformity on this matter so all schools need to seek advice locally. For visits within local authority areas, some authorities insist that children be supervised at all times whereas others allow unsupervised work in small groups provided the children are in the school grounds or, in some cases, in a local park. Some authorities do not require prior notification of fieldwork within the school district, but do ask for lists of visits on a special form submitted monthly. Others insist that requests for visits be made in advance.

There is greater uniformity regarding visits outside the authority area. Generally, permission must be sought and obtained at least seven days before the proposed visit. The teacher/pupil ratio is usually 1 to 20 with juniors and seniors, but 1 to 10 with infants. Travelling distances allowed for juniors vary between 50 and 200 miles, though no limit is usually set for secondary school pupils (fig. 8).

The teacher/pupil ratio can be as high as 1 to 40 in some areas, though 1 to 20 is more normal. Though student-teachers are counted as teachers they are not usually permitted to take out children on their own.

Many local education authorities do not allow children under twelve years of age to visit certain factories, works, or docks though there are numerous exceptions to this rule; for example certain food factories and harbours such as Southampton where conducted tours are organized.

All L.E.A.s have a blanket insurance to cover visits but many schools take out additional policies for their visits. Because of the local legal and safety requirements visits must be the concern of the school rather than the individual teacher. Sometimes the headteacher or another staff member joins the excursion, or visits are made when students are doing teaching practice; or, as in a growing number of cases, parents accompany the class visit. It is clear that if the staff consider the visits to be worthwhile, means of making them possible will be found.

Reference Material
The availability of reference material is very important for environmental studies and should therefore be a major concern of the school as a whole. However, special consideration should be given to the problem by class teachers when work is initiated.

If only a limited range and quantity of reference materials is available, the topics or interests children can follow-up are also limited. In such a situation the teacher may have to choose topics that are related to the follow-up material available. This imposes considerable restrictions on the approach, but the alternative may involve children in dabbling with a variety of interests which cannot be taken further than a simple recording stage.

Much material can also be obtained through local guides, newspaper articles, church and chapel records, the local Electricity, Gas and Water Boards, and similar sources. Also, slides of local features of significance can be assembled and tape recordings made by local residents.

With time the resources for any class will grow so that a wide range of indexed material becomes available. When this is achieved, studies can be more varied and complete, but a teacher should not be deterred at an earlier stage because of a paucity of follow-up material.

Starting Points

A teacher, with his knowledge of the age and ability of the children and his information about the environment, will choose suitable starting-points for study. The method of choice will vary. With an experienced class he will probably discuss the choice with the children. But with inexperienced classes, the starting-point is decided on by the teacher, though the specific lines of enquiry may depend upon the particular interests of the children.

One teacher considered that a study of a commercial area of the town would make a suitable theme for his class of ten-year-olds. After ensuring that plenty of resource material was available he introduced the idea to the class and discussed it with them. Their interest lay heavily on the shops in the area so that it was this particular feature that was finally studied rather than his original more general idea.

Many teachers feel it is educationally wrong for them to choose starting-points as these do not arise from the interests expressed by the children. It is immaterial who actually *chooses* the topic, as long as discussions take place before the final choice is made. In the discussions the teacher will inevitably play an important part as he will be considering the proposed feature in terms of accessibility, safety, variety and complexity. The majority of starting-points may be included under:

'**Interest studies**' such as a bunch of keys, a bench mark, a packet of sweets, a child's cardigan, a water-tap, a bicycle or a horseshoe. Such starting-points are frequently spontaneously arrived at, often for subsidiary studies within a main theme. They provide initial interests which lead on to wider topics, e.g. a child's cardigan and where it came from could lead to a study of local and world sheep farming and markets.

Single sites such as the school, a church, a mill, factory or children's playground, frequently act as starting-points. The advantages of such features for young inexperienced children are that observations can be undertaken directly on site, that they include a variety of lines for investigation and that most of it can be seen safely and easily by the children.

Area studies include wider and more complex sites such as a village, town areas, transects of various types, docks or a river. By their nature and extent they are more varied and complicated than single-site studies, thus requiring a greater variation and sophistication of analysis. Studies of this type are well suited to experienced children in upper junior, middle and lower secondary schools.

Flow Charts   Once the starting-point has been decided, possible lines of development may be considered and recorded in a flow chart. This may be produced by the teacher alone or in consultation with the children. In many cases, experienced children have themselves produced flow charts indicating the particular lines of study they would like to follow.

A simple flow chart of this type for a class of eight to nine year old children will indicate a number of different items to be studied.

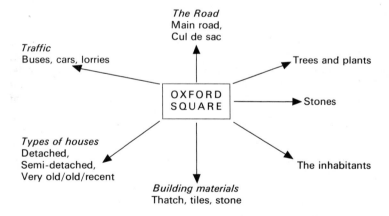

It is clear that all items noted here are concerned with the content or information provided by Oxford Square, located in a small English town. This is the form in which much project work is recorded, emphasizing concentration upon information-collecting, rather than methods of study.

For teachers another type of chart is necessary — one setting out the resources of Oxford Square. In this chart the teacher has considered the language, mathematical, artistic, scientific and locational skills that can be developed through observations within the site.

Mapping Skills
Maps and plans of Square.
Base maps using angles.
Route maps to and from school.
Plans and scale drawings of houses and their relative positions.
Use of OS maps.

Mathematical Skills
House measurements and dimensions using metres and centimetres.
Height of houses using right-angles.
Graphs — numbers in family, length of time in residence.
House types, building materials.
Traffic flows.

Language Skills
Group and class discussions. Reports from each group. Creative writing — stories and poems. Factual writing — collection and preparation of information. Questionnaires and letter writing. Use of assignment cards, reference books. Use of tape recorder for recording interviews with residents, and stories.
Exhibition of work.

OXFORD SQUARE

Change
Age of buildings.
Old maps and plans.
Interviews with residents and people with knowledge of local history.
Old photographs and records. Compare with present photographs.

Classificatory and Experimental Skills
Collection of rocks, leaves, house-types, traffic-types, etc., from Square.
Need to classify, catalogue and display collections.
Use of sampling techniques.
Experiments on types of building material, hardness, texture, etc.

Creative Skills
Pressing flowers and leaves, etc.
Collage pictures of the Square.
Painting and drawing of exterior and interior of each house. Models of houses made from variety of materials, e.g. clay, plasticine, cardboard and scrap materials.
Dolls dressed in period costumes.

When a teacher draws up a chart of this type he is clarifying his objectives and helping to ensure that purposeful work will be undertaken by children following different lines of enquiry. Although the studies are concerned with plants, traffic, houses, building materials and people, the need for observation, recording testing and interpreting is common to all of them, and is the main concern of the teacher.

Such preparatory analyses are an important element in the organization of environmental studies, emphasizing the enquiry and discovery nature of the approach.

Experienced teachers appreciate the importance of class discussions when initiating studies and throughout their later development. Records can be made on prepared forms, as in the example here showing how one study commenced with a class of ten-year-old children.

Week 1 5–9th May, 1970	Week 2 12–16th May, 1970
Material	
Old photographs of the town brought into the classroom to stimulate discussion on shops 50 years ago — how the town had changed — was this good or bad — what type of record could be made of this? Were there any records of the changes there had been. How could we find out about our town? Questionnaires? What should we ask? To what shops should the questionnaire go?	The questionnaires were typed and duplicated for pupils' visit to shops.
	I helped with the production of outlines of the shops to be made into a class frieze.
	Stories of the town in the past were read.
	General maps of town produced.
Methods (used by teacher)	
1 Class and group discussions.	1 Class together for stories of the town.
2 Visit to shopping area to select shops for close study.	2 Discussions of route maps produced by individuals.
3 Used old photographs to initiate imaginative writing on the town as it was 50 years ago.	3 Organized groups to produce cartoons of market scenes (2 m × 2·5 m).
	4 Discussion on methods of getting questionnaires answered.
Techniques (used by children)	
1 Drawing up questionnaire in groups.	1 Painting of cartoons.
2 Class decision on final questionnaire.	2 Examining written stories of the town in the past.
3 Imaginative writing based on old photographs.	3 Interviewing shopkeepers.
	4 Everybody making individual concertina booklet and inserting story and map.

This illustrates the purposeful varied activities undertaken during the first weeks of a study which continued for a term. Among other activities, discussions took place between the teacher and class, group and individuals, between the children themselves and between the children and shopkeepers.

Such discussions are important at all stages of environmental studies to improve children's powers of oral expression, though the discussions themselves need purpose. Here the discussions were aimed at answering specific questions especially related to the production of the questionnaire. If some purpose is not specified by the teacher and if no questions are forthcoming from the children, discussions become rambling and aimless.

Questionnaires

Questionnaires of the type involved in 'The street of shops' (see p. 58), together with other forms of assignment appear in many studies. They may be used at any point but tend to occur more especially in the early stages of studies as important means of collecting data. Apart from this, there is the social value of children getting used to questioning different people. Some schools develop a graded scheme of questioning whereby children first interview their class-mates, then children and teachers from other classes, followed perhaps by the caretaker and kitchen staff before they are considered sufficiently experienced to approach members of the public with either oral or written questionnaires. Of even greater value is to tape record such a progression at the different stages. Working with questionnaires children begin to realize that questions can be framed in a variety of ways in order to obtain the required information. Experienced children are able to frame questions in a number of different forms, including:

(a)   What is the name of your shop? _____

(b)   By what means are your goods delivered?_____
       – road, rail, sea or air?

(c)   When you go out shopping, do you usually:

		meat	groceries	bread	other
A	shop in Watchfield				
B	shop in Shrivenham				
C	shop at the Mobile shop				
D	shop elsewhere				

(d)   Do you think our area has enough shops?
      YES   NO   DON'T KNOW
(e)   What new shops do you think we need here?

Questionnaires involving the public should always contain an official section including the school stamp, which shows that the activity is part of school work. This ensures that those interviewed are aware that the questions have purpose and are backed by the school authorities.

Other questionnaires in the form of assignments may be developed for use within studies, and will vary in their difficulty and complexity with the age and ability of the children. For example:

Six to seven year-old children   Rocks Group
Take one of the stones we collected from the river.
1   Is it light or heavy? Guess its weight and check your answer.
2   Is it rough or smooth. Rub it against your cheek.
3   Write what colour your stone is.

Eight to nine year-old children   A Roundabout
After you have completed the traffic census answer the following questions:
1   How many vehicles of different types passed along Elm Street in both directions? Show the answer in a diagram.
2   Along which road does most traffic move?
3   Try to find out at what time of day the roundabout is busiest. What reasons can you give?

Eleven year-old children   The Bridge
Examine a large-scale map before you visit the site and try to decide why the bridge has been placed where it is.
1   Sketch the shape of the bridge and if possible take a photo-graph. What type of bridge is it? Beam, arch, suspension, moveable. Would you describe it as a skew bridge?
From your observations can you say why the bridge was built in this particular spot? Can you discover when it was constructed? Are there any signs of reconstruction or repair?
2   Find out the following information:
How is the bridge supported and strengthened?
How many spans are there?
Are there land arches on either side?

Is the river liable to flood? How do you know?

What problems do you think the builders had to meet?

Obtain all the dimensions of the bridge so that you can make a diagram or model to scale.

Notice particularly the height of the parapet. How will you find the height of the arch above the water?

3   What materials have been used in building the bridge?

Is there any pattern in the way the bricks or stone blocks have been placed? Why?

Make a diagram or rubbing of this pattern.

If stone has been used, what sizes and shapes of block has the bridge been made from?

Calculate the number required to build the whole bridge.

How have the blocks been joined together?

4   Examine one block of stone and make a note of its colour, texture, and hardness. If any broken pieces are lying around take one back with you for other experiments.

Can you say what kind of rock it is?

Find out where the rock was obtained and when it was first brought to the site.

Was the best material chosen? How would the blocks be shaped?

Does the bridge serve as a shelter or base for any creatures, or plants?

Take one section of the wall and chart all the plants and animals that you can find.

Make sketches of those you can't identify and find out what they are from your reference books.

Teachers have different views as to the role of questionnaires and work cards within environmental studies. If too much dependence is put upon them then the work can become stilted and formal. This does not mean, however, that opportunities to suggest activities by means of attractive cards should be ignored.

Grouping

Another feature that poses problems is that of group organization. Examination of the methods employed by a large number of teachers shows that there is no universal pattern. Conditions vary greatly and successful work with one group using one method may prove disastrous with other children or in different circumstances. However, despite the variations some general principles do emerge from the organizational methods employed by individual teachers.

Most teachers start with the class as a unit for both discussion and imparting information. This initial class participation is of great importance in making everyone aware of the general themes.

Further involvement of the entire class occurs where necessary throughout the study. Excursions often require children to undertake tasks as well as follow their own interests. An initial mapping excursion may specify that all children pace out a particular length of wall, identify and locate one object, make a field sketch and record their more personal observations.

Where groups have been studying features that have common characteristics, e.g. shops or factories, it is useful to co-ordinate studies on a class basis in order to reach conclusions. Groups of junior children studying several local factories have been gathered together for a class lesson by the teacher who has pointed out that raw material passes through the manufacturing processes and finishes up as a product. Similarly children studying shops have begun to appreciate the functions of producer, wholesaler, retailer and customer.

Often the local studies lead to wider environments or to earlier periods in history. When this happens the teacher usually needs to have more detailed material to link the sample study to a patch of history or a particular region. Often during the study, groups of children may report progress to the class as a whole; all the children may combine on a class frieze, map or book; and at the end of the study there will probably be some class exhibition. Thus, through a class book, a wall exhibition, a tape and slide account, or by some other means the class as a whole will illustrate its activities.

The main body of most studies is, however, undertaken through group activities, though there is little agreement on the best, and most advantageous, method of choosing the groups. Some teachers arrange their children in mixed ability groups, others in single ability groups, while many use age, interest or friendship. Even after the initial division, the groups should be flexible enough for alterations to be made.

Whatever method of group organization is adopted, teachers

encounter the problems of ensuring that children of different ages and abilities are all fully engaged in studies geared to their individual needs. Since the main object of environmental studies is the development of a range of skills for studying and communicating, it is essential that the work undertaken relates to the abilities of individual children.

In classes grouped by narrow ability bands, the more able groups will use and develop a wide range of study skills as they follow their lines of enquiry. The less able groups, probably with more direction from the teacher, will also contribute to the general theme though by studies concentrating upon a narrower range of skills. For example, in one study a group of able children examined maps, pictures, written and oral accounts to enable them to make a model of a crossroads illustrating conditions in 1850 and 1970 together with their proposals for future traffic flow in the area. A less able group in the same class studied various types of tyres, visited garages and undertook simple tests — all the experiences were talked and written about. Some less experienced teachers in this situation might have urged the less able to undertake the model making and painting. The concentration upon language development was geared to the weaknesses in the children concerned.

Another problem to be found within mixed ability groups is that the more able children frequently act as leaders, though all teachers should bear in mind that those of high intelligence are not necessarily the strongest personalities. Teachers need to be aware of the dangers where the less able within the group are constantly allocated the less demanding tasks rather than being involved in more purposeful work. For example, where language ability is limited children may be more able at drawing maps, making sketches or taking photographs, and through these activities a greater use of language can arise.

Problems of coping with wide ability ranges are especially marked in small schools where children from seven to eleven years are found in one class. There are mutual advantages in having groups within which able and less experienced children can work together, but teachers must be aware of the fact that study skills have recognizable stages in their development, and that children can cope only so far as their experience provides. In a class study involving a belt transect the oldest children may appreciate a complete map of the zone, be able to classify plants and buildings according to a number of criteria and undertake tests involving two or three variables; but the younger children may be capable only of making a plan of one building, recognizing simple resemblances between specimens and conducting only the simplest tests.

Provided that teachers are clear as to the objectives of the work, mixed ability groups of four to six children appear to be the most suitable group arrangement. However, many teachers use a variety of arrangements; there are instances of classes commencing their studies with mixed ability groups but, as the studies have developed, children have moved or have been moved from these to form new single ability groups and to undertake individual investigations.

An important item in the activities is each group's report to the whole class. In these reports it is important that children illustrate the ways in which they have conducted their studies, rather than concentrate upon what they have discovered. Such reports are useful not only in linking the different aspects of the study but also in helping the reporting groups to clarify their thoughts and present their contributions clearly and concisely. Here again it is important that reports should not be undertaken only by a select few; all children should participate in the reporting. It is the improvement of children's confidence and ability in communicating with others by words, diagrams and audio-visual machines that is the main purpose of the reports.

Teachers and Children

In all aspects of environmental studies teachers are at the centre as organizers, helpers and, at times, leaders (figs. 9 and 10). Children need help in their studies and the skilful teacher knows when this help is needed.

The relationship of the teacher to the children will depend to some degree on the school organization. Most primary schools give one teacher the responsibility for the whole environmental studies field with his class, though the work may be seen as part of a school scheme.

In some schools, especially those built to an open-plan design, an environmental studies specialist works from a single base used by all. Children use the environmental studies area either at will or during the block of time allocated to them.

Other primary schools use various forms of co-operative teaching. These forms vary: there may be co-operation only in the planning of studies where specialist knowledge and experience is pooled by the staff in preparation; or there may be co-operation between teachers, sharing the responsibility for a number of children, in particular curriculum fields.

A variety of forms of organization also occurs in the middle years of schooling. With less able and remedial classes one teacher often acts as a class-teacher for a large part of the curriculum, which is not divided on the basis of subject specializations.

With children of average ability several teachers co-operate in a central theme on the basis of their own special interests. Frequently within such co-operation there are opportunities which will allow children to develop subject specializations at a later stage. History, biology and geography teachers may combine in the study of different aspects of a site or theme, and in doing so will specify particular skills and concepts which are related to later specialist studies.

Within all of these patterns of organization teachers must devise their own methods of achieving their educational aims and objectives. An environmental studies approach is not an easy teaching method: it requires hard work in the provision of resources, the organization and conduct of excursions, and above all in the constant contact with children as individuals. In the process of using the environment as a resource for learning by children, teachers themselves are altered. The examination of ordinary life around them develops added interests and insights into the pattern of their world. One of the great dangers facing all teachers is boredom through familiarity with school routine. Studies based upon ever-changing environments help to combat this tired state of mind. Awareness of the nature and quality of environments is not only a requirement for children but also for their teachers.

Conclusion

This book attempts to provide some guidance for teachers in primary and middle schools in a curriculum field that has too long suffered from imprecision.

In formulating the approach it has been necessary to give a structured character to the work undertaken by children learning under a succession of different teachers. Rigid adherence to a preconceived scheme can kill the character and value of child-based activities relying on interest and spontaneity, and a course has to be found between unorganized chaos and sterile programmes.

The structure specified is a guide to schools wishing to use the environment as an educational resource. Local features and interests provide the activities for the children, but the teacher is helped to see these against a framework of methods of observation and analysis. Teachers lacking specialist training in this curriculum field need some context within which they can see the relevance and purpose of their children's activities. The work must be considered as a normal part of school activity, not a series of occasional interludes in the school programme. Experience has shown the feasibility of the approach where headteachers and staff combine to undertake the organization and provide the necessary resources.

Structures tied to a rigid framework of concepts are rejected in favour of a body of skills which grows as the children develop. The aim of environmental studies is the development of adaptable, perceptive and confident children who can grasp a wide range of ideas and absorb information. It also fosters a well-balanced attitude to people and the quality of the environments in which they live and for which they will have responsibility.

Appendix 1   Useful Addresses

The following addresses are of organizations that are able to provide assistance to schools. In most instances titles indicate the nature of the material available. A charge covering the cost of production and postage is made in most instances.

Museums and Archives
The British Museum, Great Russell Street, London, WC1
The Science Museum, South Kensington, London, SW7
The National Maritime Museum, Greenwich, London, SE10
Public Record Office, Chancery Lane, London, WC2A ILK
British Rail Archives, 66 Porchester Road, London, W2
The National Museum of Wales, Cathays Park, Cardiff
The National Library of Wales, Aberystwyth, Cardiganshire
Business Archives Council, Ormonde House, 63 Queen Victoria
  Street, London, EC4
Commonwealth Institute, Kensington High Street, London, W8
Geological Museum, Exhibition Road, London, SW7
London Museum, Kensington Palace, London, W8
Imperial War Museum, Lambeth Road, London, SE1
Natural History Museum, Cromwell Road, London, SW7
Victoria & Albert Museum, Cromwell Road, London, SW7

Most County and Borough Councils now provide an archives service and in a number of cases have museums which can assist schools. Pamphlet No. 62 entitled *County Records* published by the Historical Association, 59a Kennington Park Road, London, SE11, provides a comprehensive list of authorities that are able to offer facilities.

Maps
The Director General, Ordnance Survey, Romsey Road, Maybush,
  Southampton, SO9 4DH

Land Use Maps
E. Stanford, Ltd., 12 Long Acre, London, WC2E 9LD

Aerial Photographs
Aerofilms & Aero Pictorial Ltd., 4 Albermarle Street, London,
W1X 3HF
Meridian Airways, Commerce Way, Lancing, Sussex
H. Tempest (Cardiff) Ltd., 31 Clare Road, Cardiff, CF1 7QP

Fairey Air Survey Ltd., 24 Bruton Street, London, WIX 3HF
Dr. J. K. St. Joseph, University Curator in Aerial Photography, Selwyn College, Cambridge

Government Departments
Sectional Catalogues of Government Publications from Her Majesty's Stationery Offices:
P.O. Box 569, London, SE1
13a Castle Street, Edinburgh, 2
109 St. Mary Street, Cardiff
Brazenose Street, Manchester
50 Fairfax Street, Bristol, 1
35 Smallbrook, Ringway, Birmingham, 5
80 Chichester Street, Belfast, 1
Central Office of Information, Hercules Row, Westminster Bridge Road, London, SE1
Ministry of Public Buildings and Works, Lambeth Bridge House, Albert Embankment, London, SE1
The Forestry Commission, 25 Savile Row, London, W1X 1AA
Ministry of Agriculture, Agricultural Censuses and Surveys Branch, Epsom Road, Guildford, Surrey

Public Utilities
Public Relations Department, GPO Headquarters, St. Martins le Grand, London, EC1
Chief Publicity Officer, British Transport Commission, 222 Marylebourne Road, London, NW1
Publications Officer, The Gas Council, 1 Grosvenor Place, London, SW7
Education Officer, Electricity Council, Winsley Street, London, W1
National Parks Commission, 1 Cambridge Gate, Regents Park, London, NW1

Private Organizations and Firms
Association of Agriculture, 78 Buckingham Gate, London, SW1
Field Studies Council, 9 Devereux Court, Strand, London, WC2R 3JJ
British Waterworks Association, 34 Park Street, London, W1
The National Trust, 42 Queen Anne's Gate, London, SW1
Inland Waterways Association, 4 Emerald Street, London, WC1

The Petroleum Information Bureau, 29 New Bond Street, London, W1

British Iron and Steel Federation, Steel House, Tothill Street, London, SW1

Glass Manufacturers' Federation, 19 Portland Place, London, W1

The Natural Rubber Development Board, Market Buildings, Mark Lane, London, EC3

Kelly's Directories Ltd., Neville House, Eden Street, Kingston-upon-Thames, Surrey

Educational Aids Bureau, Tate and Lyle, Ltd., 21 Mincing Lane, London, EC3

The Ceylon Tea Centre, 22 Regent Street, Piccadilly Circus, London, SW1

Education Department, National Milk Publicity Council, Melbourne House, Aldwych, London, WC2

The Education Department, British Manmade Fibres Federation, Bridgewater House, 58 Whitworth Street, Manchester, 1

The International Wool Secretariat, Dorland House, 18–20 Regent Street, London, SW1

Cotton Board, 3 Alberton Street, Manchester, 3

The following firms are producing very useful local and regional books, together with reprints of out-of-print works. Details can be obtained on request.

S.R. Publishers, Ltd., East Ardsley, Wakefield, Yorkshire, or 17 Denbigh Street, London, SW1

David & Charles (Holdings) Ltd., South Devon House, Newton Abbot, Devon

A comprehensive list of Museums and Art Galleries entitled *Museums and Galleries in Great Britain and Ireland* is published annually (July) by Index Publishers, 30 Finsbury Square, London, EC2.

National Organizations

Centre for Environmental Studies, 5 Cambridge Terrace, Regents Park, London, NW1 4JL

Civic Trust, 17 Carlton House Terrace, London, SW1

Council for Environmental Education, c/o Royal Society of Arts, John Adam Street, London, WC2N 6AJ

Countryside Commission, 1 Cambridge Gate, Regents Park, London, NW1 24JY

Geographical Association, 343 Fulwood Road, Sheffield, SI0 3BP

Nature Conservancy, 19 Belgrave Square, London, W1

National Rural and Environmental Studies Association, General Secretary, D. G. Alexander, County Hall, March, Cambs.

Society for Environmental Education, Secretary, G. C. Martin, 16 Trinity Road, Enderby, Leicester, LE9 5BU

Appendix 2   Bibliography

General Background Reading

Arvill, R. *Man and Environment* Penguin 1967

Bloom, B. S. *Taxonomy of Educational Objectives — Handbook I — Cognitive Domain 1956, Handbook II — Affective Domain* Longmans 1964

Blyth, W. A. L. *English Primary Education, Vols 1 and 2* Routledge and Kegan Paul 1965

Brown, M. and Precious, N. *The Integrated Day in the Primary School* Ward Lock Educational 1968

Bruner, J. S. *The Process of Education* Vintage Books 1960

Bruner, J. S. *Toward a Theory of Instruction* Harvard University Press 1967

Bruner, J. S. *On Knowing — Essays for the Left Hand* Harvard University Press 1962

Camm, A. A. and Sund, R. B. *Teaching Science Through Discovery* C. E. Merrill Pub. Co., 1970

Christian, G. *Tomorrow's Countryside* John Murray 1966

Dearden, . F. *The Philosophy of Primary Education* Routledge and Kegan Paul 1968

Doncaster, I. *Discovering Man's Habitat* National Froebel Foundation 1963

Eggbeston, S. J. *The Social Context of the School* Routledge and Kegan Paul 1967

Gardner, D. E. M. *Experiment and Tradition in Primary Schools* Methuen 1965

Gittins, C. *Primary Education in Wales* Central Advisory Council for Education (Wales), H.M.S.O. 1967

Heath, O. V. S. *Investigation by Experiment* E. Arnold 1970

Hopkins, M. F. S. *Learning Through the Environment* Longmans 1968

Lovell, K. *The Growth of Basic Mathematical and Scientific Concepts in Children* University of London Press 1965

Neagley, R. L. and Dean Evans, N. *Handbook for Effective Curriculum Development* Prentice Hall Inc. 1967

Nicholson, M. *The Environmental Revolution* Hodder & Stoughton 1970

Piaget, J. and Inhelder, B. *The Growth of Logical Thinking* Routledge and Kegan Paul 1958

Piaget, J. and Inhelder, B. *The Child's Conception of Space* Routledge and Kegan Paul 1956

Plowden, B. *Children and their Primary Schools* Central Advisory
Council for Education (England), Vol. 1, H.M.S.O. 1967
Sigel, I. E. and Hooper, F. H. *Logical Thinking in Children* Holt,
Rinehart and Winston 1969
Stewart, W. A. C. and McCann, W. P. *The Educational Innovators*
Macmillan 1967
Stott, L. H. *Child Development* Holt, inehart and Winston 1967
Taba, H. *Curriculum Development — Theory and Practice*
Harcourt, Brace and World, Inc. 1962
UNESCO *The Study of Environment in School* International
Bureau of Education, Geneva, UNESCO, Place de Fontenery,
Paris 1968
Wiseman, S. *Intelligence and Ability* Penguin Books 1967

Teaching Environmental Studies
Few books deal specifically with an environmental studies
approach, but the following are a selection of the more useful
guides for teachers.
Archer, J. E. and Dalton, T. H. *Fieldwork in Geography* Batsford
1968
Armstrong, J. R. and Hopkins, P. G. H. *Local Studies* W.E.A.,
Temple House, 27 Portman Square, London, W1, 1955
Allen, G., Brown, V., Southern, H. and Tube, E. *Scientific Interests
in the Primary School* National Froebel Foundation
Boon, G. *Townlook* Pergamon Press 1969
Briault and Shave *Geography in and out of School* Harrap
Burston, W. H. and Green, C. W. *Handbook for History Teachers*
Methuen Co. 1967
Celoria, F. *Teach Yourself Local History* E.U.P. 1958
Cleland, D. M., Rees Davies, B. and Hann, D. W. *Exploring Science
in the Primary School* Collier-Macmillan 1967
Dilke, M. S. *Field Studies for Schools, Vol. 1* Rivingtons, London
1968
Douch *Local History and the Teacher* Routledge and Kegan Paul
Emmison, F. G. *Introduction to Archives* BBC Publications
Emmison, F. G. *Archives and Local History* Methuen 1966
Ennever, L. *Science 5/13 Project — Materials* Macdonald
Educational
Ford, V. E. *How to Begin your Fieldwork. 1 — Woodland, 2 —
Seashore* John Murray

Glasspool, F. F. and Laybourn, K. *Foundations of Science* University of London Press 1965

Haddon, J. *Local Geography* G. Philips & Son 1964

Hoskins, W. G. *Fieldwork in Local History* Faber & Faber Ltd 1967

Hopkins, M. F. S. *Learning Through the Environment* Longmans 1968

James, A. *Simple Science Experiments* Schofield & Sons

Kirby, M. *Meet Me in Trafalgar Square* Schoolmaster Pub. Co. 1968

Lines, C. and Bolwell, L. *Teaching Environmental Studies* Ginn & Co. 1971

Masterton, T. H. *Environmental Studies – A Concentric Approach* Oliver & Boyd 1969

Moser, C. A. and Kalton, G. *Survey Methods in Social Investigations* Heinemann 1971

Perkins, W. H. *The Place of Science in Primary Education* British Association for the Advancement of Science 1962

Perry, G. A., Jones, E. and Hammersley, D. A. *The Teachers' Handbook for Environmental Studies* Blandford Press Ltd. 1968

Pike, E. R. *Human Documents of the Industrial Revolution in Britain* Allen & Unwin Ltd. 1966

Pugh *How to Write a Parish History* Allen & Unwin Ltd.

Pemberton, P. H. (ed.) *Geography in Primary Schools* The Geographical Association 1970

igg, J. B. *A Textbook of Environmental Studies for School Scientists* Constable 1968

Sankey, J. *A Guide to Field Biology* Longmans 1967

Sauvain, P. A. *A Geographical Field Study Companion* Hulton Educational Publishers 1966

Spoczynska, J. O. I. *Practical Fieldwork for the Young Naturalist* F. Muller 1967

Watts, D. G. *Environmental Studies* Routledge and Kegan Paul 1969

Wheeler, K. S. and Harding, M. *Geographical Fieldwork – A Handbook* Blond Educational 1965

Young, I. V. *Farm Studies in Schools* Association of Agriculture, 78 Buckingham Gate, London, SW1 (1968)

Handbook for Expeditions Brathay Exploration Group, The Geographical Magazine 1971

Rural Studies in Secondary Schools Schools Council Working Paper 24 1969

Leicestershire Landscapes Leicestershire Association for Local Geographical Studies Blond Educational 1968

School Projects in Natural History Devon Trust for Nature Conservation, Slapton Ley Field Centre, Kingsbridge, S. Devon

Leaflets and Pamphlets School Natural Science Society M. J. Wootton, 44 Claremont Gardens, Upminster, Essex, M14 IDN

Study Geography Series Longmans 1969

Primary Education in Scotland HMSO 1965

Schools and the Countryside HMSO Pamphlet No. 35, 1958

Source Book for Geography Teaching UNESCO, Longmans Green & Co.

A Selection of Suitable Reference Material for Children

Allen, G. and Denslow, J. *The Clue Books* O.U.P. 1970

Bell, G. *What Happens When series* Oliver & Boyd 1970

Blakeway, M. *People of the Past series* O.U.P. 1962

Catherall, E. A. and Holt, P. N. *Working with Weather* Bailey Bros & Swinfen 1962

Clarke, M. *Observe and Learn series* Rupert Hart-Davis Educational 1967

Copus, C. and Lather, B. *Photographic Work Cards* W. Claves & Sons Ltd. 1971

Dark, I. *Science is Fun series* Pergamon

Derwent, L. (ed.) *Exploring Science series* Burke 1966

Doncaster, I. *Evidence in Pictures series* Longmans 1966

Edwards, R. P. A. *The Changing Scene Series* Burke, London, 1970

Finch, I. *Town and Country series* Longmans 1969

James, G. and Walford, R. (eds) *On the Spot Geographies* Longmans 1968

Lines, C. J. and Bolwell, L. H. *Discovering Your Environment series* Ginn & Co. 1969

Milburn, D. *A First Book of Geology* Basil Blackwell 1967

Nuttall, K. *Services We Use series* Longmans

Nye, T. M. *Parish Church Architecture* Batsford 1965

Oakley, K. P. and Muir-Wood, H. M. *The Succession of Life Through Geological Time* British Museum 1959

Owen, R. (ed.) *Let's Look At series* F. Muller 1965

Perry, G. A. (ed.) *Approaches to Environmental Studies series* Blandford Press 1969

Rawle, F. and Freeman, T. *Young Investigator series* Schofield & Simms 1963

Razzell, A. G. and Watts, K. G. O. *Mathematical Topics series* Rupert Hart-Davis Educational 1970

Reeves, M. (Gen. ed.) *Then and There series* Longmans

Rowland, K. *Finding Out About Science series* Rupert Hart-Davis Educational 1962

Showers, P. *Let's Read and Find Out series* Black

Sauvain, P. A. *Discovery Series, Books 1–6* Macmillan 1970

Scarfe, H. G. *As We Were series* Longmans

Sealey, L. *Basic Skills in Learning* Nelson 1970

Usherwood, S. and Usherwood, H. *History from Familiar Things* Ginn & Co. 1969

A Little Guide in Colour series P. Hamlyn, London

Discovering series Shire Publications, Gubblecote Cross, Tring, Herts

Exploring Nature, Books 1–6 E. J. Arnold

Life and Science series Methuen & Co.

Junior Science Books F. Muller

Macdonald Junior Reference Library Macdonald Educational

Make and Find Out series Macmillan

On the Spot Geographies Longmans 1968

Stand and Stare Books Methuen & Co.

The Local Search series Routledge and Kegan Paul

Young Naturalist series, Books 1–11 A. & C. Black

Young Specialist Looks At series Burke, London

This is Your World series, Books 1–5 Holmes McDougall Ltd. 1971

Get to Know series Methuen & Co.

Index

1 0 MAR 1986

1 8 MAY 1986

5 MAY 1986

9 MAR 1987

2 1 MAY 1987

17 FEB 1988

2 6 FEB 1990

1 4 MAR 1990

2 3 MAR 1990

1 6 MAY 1990

1 5 MAY 1990

4 JUN 1990

-5 JUN 1990

2 5 NOV 1992

2 6 NOV 1992

2 4 JUN 1993

2 3 JUN 1993

2 0 APR 1994

1 3 MAY 1994

2 6 MAY 1994

JUN 1994

JUN 1994

Class No. 372.83   Acc. No. 38644

COLÁISTE OIDEACHAIS
MHUIRE GAN SMÁL,
LUIMNEACH.

WITHDRAWN
FROM STOCK